27062

N.N.

Sea Cliff Climbing in Britain

Sea Cliff Climbing in Britain

John Cleare & Robin Collomb

Constable London

First published in Great Britain 1973 by
Constable & Company Ltd, 10 Orange Street, London WC2H 7EG

Copyright © 1973 by John Cleare & Robin Collomb

ISBN 0 09 458220 3

Printed by Ebenezer Baylis and Son Ltd, Leicester and London.

Contents

Illustrations

Maps of the various coastal regions appear at the beginning of each chapter section.

Introduction

As an island race the British people are accustomed to fine coastal scenery. Most of us do not give it a second thought except at holiday times. It is no accident that our shores are bulwarked for long distances by cliffs composed of rocks ranging from the oldest to the youngest, and from the softest to the hardest known to man. The story of geology from the earliest times is told in the complex profile of our coastal boundaries.

British sea cliffs deserve the universal accord of ranking among the finest and most varied in the world. They have been eroded and carved by the sea and aerial elements into fantastic shapes, and may only be wanting in great height when compared with rival scenery in other countries.

Then in these islands, so small against the size of mainland continents, we are doubly fortunate in having rugged mountains and splendid sea cliffs situated within a reasonable distance of each other; sometimes both can be shared in the same moment. But in the sport of mountaineering the two have generally been kept apart. As the country moved into the industrial revolution of the nineteenth century, so the shoreline became reserved for relaxation and holidaymaking. About fifty years later small groups of people started climbing rockfaces in the mountainous regions. There they remained, their numbers growing slowly, loathing the leisure atmosphere pervading the beaches, while roots were planted and traditions established. In moving from one coastal area to another the change we shall describe represents the first and only significant departure from habitual climbing grounds to come upon the mountaineering scene in Britain. There are signs that it may have far-reaching consequences.

In this book we have endeavoured to trace the course of climbing on the sea cliffs of Britain in three ways. By looking at the origins of this special branch of a pastime traditionally confined to mountain areas; by describing the story of exploration up to the present day; by commenting on the nature and quality of the climbing that sea cliffs provide. If we discount the casual overtures made by climbers over the years, sustained activity on British sea cliffs is only twenty years old. Yet already it can be said with some certainty that ideas in the new pastime are diverging from normal climbing patterns. A separate, perhaps more specialised – or at any rate freshly motivated – pastime could be the result. We are less sure that climbers in general will be able to enjoy the new as they enjoy the "old"; or whether they will want to. Already the first sizable generation of sea cliff climbers has emerged. They learnt to climb on sea-washed rock and spend most of their leisure hours on the coast. Sea cliffs are beginning to attract more young people to mountaineering than could otherwise reach the ranks of the pastime – notably in the south-west, where there are no mountains. A situation can be foreseen where these climbers may for some years, or even decades, confine themselves to local sea cliffs, as many did on the gritstone during the 1920s and 1930s – but for different reasons. Poverty is unlikely to be the explanation in the future why climbers may not set their sights on greener but more distant pastures. Contentment with a regional and more personal or domestic role could be the answer. Less travelling, effort and possibly planning are involved in sea cliff climbing, although in the last respect techniques are so new that experience and improvement of them still have a long way to go before the climber can relax in confidence.

In the North the vogue for sea cliff climbing has developed for a variety of reasons. Frustration is a prominent one. At present sea cliffs are regarded, quite properly, as second best – that is unless you are a natural sea cliff climber. They are climbed because the rock is steep, possibly quite good, and presents bold features that are obvious challenges to the cragsman. But the sea and the problems it may present against the cliff face are avoided as far as possible. Climbers have been driven to the coast when routes on their favourite rockfaces in the mountains have become too crowded, when rain, wind or snow have repelled them, or when in desperation virgin rock on which to make new routes must be found. Yet none of these reasons typify the outlook of the habitual sea cliff climber as he seems to exist in the 1970s.

Scotland is a special case. A few cliffs near built-up areas have been developed by local climbers, but the magnificent coastal precipices of the North have scarcely been touched. Any attempt on these calls for expedition planning and seige tactics, as they are well beyond the bounds of a weekend jaunt. In the North of Scotland efforts have been concentrated on the famous pillars of Old Red and Torridonian Sandstone standing off remote coasts. A televised ascent of the Old Man of Hoy focused attention on the possibilities for climbing Scottish stacks, and the thirty or so tackled to date mark only a beginning.

We have not attempted to cover all the potentially worthwhile sea cliffs in Britain, and Ireland* has been omitted altogether. We can reflect soberly that the sheer length and complexity of coastline forming these

*A country with only a small mountaineering movement, Eire has sea cliffs higher than any in the rest of Britain, many of them totally unexplored. Slieve League is reckoned as the finest ocean cliff in Europe, approx. 1,800 ft. high.

islands have no equal for creating curiosity and interest. The unsurpassed range of scenic contrasts would take a lifetime to explore and appreciate fully. Our guidelines have been laid down by considerations of popularity and the state of development on cliffs at the present time. All the same this has still left us with the task of travelling all the ground between Land's End and John o' Groats, not to mention the islands further North and St Kilda in the grey Atlantic.

With mountains crowded into the northern parts of England and Wales, sea cliffs become progressively less important as we work our way up the country from the English and Bristol Channels. For the first time in domestic mountaineering the South has taken an original initiative against the long-held entrenchments of the North. It has found other locations and other reasons for rock climbing. No claims can be made for emulating the "spirit of the mountains", as it clearly does not apply. The attractions of sea cliffs for climbing are no less complicated than those held for mountains. The sea constitutes a major part of them – an inscrutable element with as many moods as the human mind that regards it. But the duplication of technical applications on rock can be readily appreciated. Another fairly evident quality is entertainment; this might be termed the coastal equivalent of "interest" as it can be defined for mountains. This entertainment is plainly more fundamental than mountaineering interest; that is to say less abstract; and you enjoy it more naturally because of a seascape locale. Conventional attainments as in regular sports would seem to have scope for advancement in some varieties of sea cliff climbing – in traversing and coasteering. The first of these is already a "great game" in the pastime, with its own problems and techniques. Played in a lower key, the second could attract thousands ignorant at the outset of all mountaineering principles.

For the moment sea cliffs are attractive for their technicalities and breath of change from the mountain atmosphere. Their ultimate impact on the course of mountaineering in Britain we may be able to judge with accuracy by the end of this decade.

Historical Note
by Peter Biven

Sea cliff climbing as a sport, and distinct from activities such as mining or collecting birds-eggs, is of Victorian origin. Most of the earliest references are to the chalk of South-East England. The pioneers – famous alpinists such as Mummery, Tyndall, Whymper and the notorious black magician, Aleister Crowley – were practising for Alpine mountaineering and treated the chalk as though it were ice or snow. Crowley climbed Etheldreda's Pinnacle on Beachy Head – a remarkable achievement and in concept years ahead of its time. Others were not unaware of the peculiar hazards of chalk climbing. As early as 1869 Tyndall wrote of Swanage, "These cliffs provided me with quite sensational risks – there are bits on these places as dangerous as anything in the Alps". But after the turn of the century the mountaineering world unaccountably seemed to lose interest, and for many years hardly anyone climbed on our chalk cliffs. There are, however, signs that the wheel may be turning full circle: Beachy Head has been climbed, mainly with pegs and with the protection of a very long top-rope. Robin Collomb climbed one of the Needles on the Isle of Wight from a clinker dinghy in 1951. There have been sporadic attempts on the other Needles and Old Harry on the other side of the Solent. Devon climbers have recently completed some very high grade chalk traverses at Beer in East Devon. But so far the technique required for dealing with flints which pull out precipitately and the crumbling nature of the chalk has proved elusive.

In the far West, in Cornwall, the earliest recorded sea cliff climb was made in 1858 by Sir Leslie Stephen – an event which pre-dates much of the pioneer mountain rock climbing. But it wasn't until 1887 that Longstaff began traversing parts of the North Cornwall coast and made the boat trip to Lundy where he recorded an ascent of the Gannet Rock – a gaunt sea stack which features in his book. He also climbed on St James's Stone near the famous Devil's Slide.

About the turn of the century A. W. Andrews, the father of sea cliff climbing, began an association with Cornwall which was to last for more than half a century. His early explorations were nearly all horizontal, because the tops of the cliffs, in all but a few places, have an overburden of mud and loose stones which discouraged the early pioneers. This development, which is now known as traversing, has a distinctly different character and requires skills such as swimming, lassoing, a knowledge of tide and wave-patterns and the ability to deal with angry fulmars and cormorants attacking from above, and sharks, jellyfish and congers from below.

In the early decades of this century it was the sea cliffs in the South of England, almost exclusively, which received attention. Mallory, Winthrop Young, Odell, Shadbolt and many others sampled the rough granite of the South-West, but most were in holiday mood and developments were leisurely. In 1912 Shadbolt tried a bold experiment with portable footholds – employing carefully selected limpets on Channel Island slabs – but they stubbornly refused to co-operate. During the 1920s and 1930s sea cliff climbing all but died out, probably because economic factors were a severe restriction on the small numbers climbing, and those who could get away went to the mountains. But the war changed all that: the military came to Cornwall with the express purpose of training raiding parties as quickly as possible in the art of rock climbing. For obvious reasons the bulk of the Army was concentrated in the South and therefore the superb granite cliffs were extremely accessible, thus cutting down approach time. Another positive factor was that the mild weather permitted high grade climbing, with warm fingers, to be taught at all seasons. Not only do sea cliff climbers claim to have introduced climbing in rubbers to mountain-eers as Andrews did in 1912 on Lliwedd, but the requirements of the military, in training for surprise attack, resulted in the introduction of the moulded rubber "Commando" sole – first used in this country on sea cliffs.

A solitary giant, Menlove Edwards, who has a claim to be the first amphibious climber, explored a great deal of the Cornish coast towards the end of the war. He once spent a week girdle traversing a Norwegian fiord carrying everything on his back.

After the war, with petrol rationing until 1950, few climbers were able to get further than a bus-ride away from their home town. When the boom began most followed the pre-war patterns and continued to develop the mountain crags, the gritstone edges and the limestone of the Peak. The introduction of conscription was to have a significant effect on these patterns. Many National Servicemen were posted to camps on the fringes of our coasts: particularly those who joined the Royal Marines, the Navy and radar establishments in the Air Force. Tom Patey was a Marine doctor in Devon during the fifties and made some characteristically bold climbs on the North Devon coast and elsewhere at this time. Peter Biven began the exploration of the Whin Sill sea cliffs of Northumberland in 1954, to be followed a year later by concentrated efforts on Bosigran and the granite of Cornwall. Brilliant service climbers such as Deacon, Goodier, Banks and Stevenson began lacing the fierce cliffs of Land's End with intimidating routes. And by 1958 Barry Annette was forcing some very hard lines at

Swanage in Dorset.

By the early sixties there was a dedicated group, still fairly small, of regular coastal climbers who had discovered that the problems and techniques of sea cliff climbing differ in many respects and often very greatly from those of British mountain rock climbing. The problems of access are generally greater; often the view from the clifftop is restricted and climbers may well miss essential features such as caves or roofed-zawns. Roping down is often hazardous as many sea cliffs are convex and would commit the climber to a laborious return up the rope by prusik or jumar. In at least one recent case, during the early exploration of Cilan on the Lleyn Peninsula, a climber lost consciousness whilst spinning uncontrollably at the end of a hawser-laid rope, to recover at the shock of falling in the sea. A dinghy is often used to reach off-shore islands or stacks but it is more common for a member of the party to strip and swim, if the distance is not too great, then to fix a Tyrolean rope traverse for the rest. Caves are often difficult to enter and form effective barriers to the continuity of a traverse – some impassable at high tide or offering extremely difficult rock climbing – for example the great cave under the Old Redoubt at Berry Head, Torbay. These problems and many others, such as seaweed, acorn barnacles and other razor-sharp shells, wave-worn rock – highly polished and treacherous underfoot, problems of exposure and the "wet/cold spiral", the objective danger of being washed off by a powerful swell, all this and much besides means that a landcliff climber requires a reasonable apprenticeship in order to learn these new skills. The ability to judge wave patterns for instance is not learned overnight. So when the great "gold rush" of 1964 to Gogarth started, climbing pubs began to echo with terrible tales of "epics" – many of which were probably avoidable. One of them involving the comparatively rare occurrence of the freak wave is worth mentioning. Sir Francis Chichester states that there is a physical law in which one wave in every 300,000 is roughly four times the height of all the others. It may well be that it was such a wave that struck Joe Brown when he was tied to a peg at the foot of a new route on Gogarth; the wave struck, leaving him staked to the cliff, at one point some twenty-five feet under the water. This is a fairly severe test of a second's ability to belay his leader.

The movement to Gogarth, seen in the context of the history of sea cliff climbing, was not seminal, although it did precipitate a sudden refocus of interest in sea cliffs all over the country. At first it was regarded as a great new crag, with tremendous potential, that just happened to be by the sea. It was only very much later, after the first fiercely competitive wave had spent itself, that the traverses were completed. Exploration of sea cliffs is normally done in reverse order.

After the mid-sixties there was frenzied activity on all points of the compass: the colossal potential of South Wales, from Gower to St David's Head, began to be realised. Talbot, Mortlock, Perrin and many others were in the vanguard. Gabbro, Dolerite, Sandstone and Limestone in profusion, each wave-washed into characteristic formations, were the hunting grounds of an older Llanberis generation, now disinherited by the tremendous numbers of young climbers, rock-hungry and weaning themselves on the mountain classics. Others looked to the Lleyn Peninsula and recorded some hair-raising lines through the roofs of Cilan – battling with sea birds, tidal currents and unfamiliar rock. Whilst the explorations at Gogarth continued into areas previously scanned by television cameras for the first of the sea cliff "spectaculars", not far away at Little Orme some tentative and traumatic explorations revealed a far larger cliff than many had realised. This too was soon to receive an onslaught and is now established as a major limestone sea cliff with its share of long, intimidating routes, though unlikely ever to be popular.

Lakeland climbers, although having nothing of the quality of a Gogarth, have recently developed the sandstone of St Bees Head. Unhappily the geology of the area is such that it is highly unlikely that sea cliffs will provide much other than an occasional bad weather diversion from the mountain crags. But not so over the border.

In 1967 the television programme on the Old Man of Hoy brought an awareness among climbers that there was another and somewhat different facet of sea cliffs which had been somewhat overlooked: the sea stack. The virgin summit has long since disappeared among our home mountains – even among the Alps. To do genuine explorations as such one needs to travel very far. But stacks are, for the most part, unclimbed summits, which were the original objectives of mountaineering. And numerous possibilities surround our coast. Climbing these may often be far from straightforward – many are vertical and undercut at the base by the sea. Sometimes the quality of the rock is suspect; so new and ingenious tactics are being devised. One stack at Ladram Bay in East Devon thwarted all efforts, even with a bow and arrow, until it was discovered that builders' nails, set in the mud seams of the sandstone, provided adequate protection. On another it was found that by the loan of a kite from a child on the beach, a corlene line could be flown over the top. But no doubt, in the course of time when the ethics of this sport have become less fluid, this may be considered improper.

By the end of the sixties, stacks from Land's End to far beyond John o' Groats were having rough cairns built on their bird-limed summits. Some had no firm rock on which to fix a descent abseil, so that two climbers simultaneously rope down opposite faces – yet another example of safe

15

expedients being used, uniquely, by sea cliff climbers.

Some stacks are elegant and slender like the Elugug Needle in Pembrokeshire or the Devil's Chimney on Lundy: others are broad and lumpy, like battleships riding at anchor. But they all have an elusive quality which is extraordinarily seductive, a quality of remoteness and inaccessibility which, for most climbers, is a welcome feature. And offshore islands which have to be approached by boat, like those of Hanjague and Men a' Vaur in the Scillies, offer unlimited opportunities for traversing and the ascents of stacks and isolated pinnacles. The rising and falling of the tides and the ever-changing background of the sea, coupled with the myriad distractions of the shoreline – caverns, creeks, crystals; flotsam and strangely-formed sea and time-worn rocks, make sea cliffs fascinating to explore and delightful to be among.

1 Chalk Cliffs

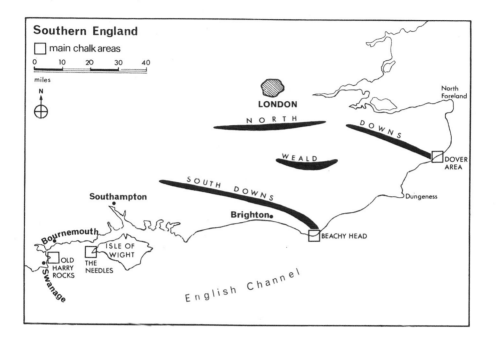

Southern England

main chalk areas

0   10   20   30   40
miles

N

LONDON

NORTH

DOWNS

WEALD

SOUTH DOWNS

Southampton

Brighton

North Foreland

DOVER AREA

Dungeness

BEACHY HEAD

Bournemouth

ISLE OF WIGHT

OLD HARRY ROCKS

THE NEEDLES

Swanage

English Channel

History records that Britain as a maritime nation is best remembered
by those arriving at and leaving its shores by prominent landmarks
dotting the coastline. Especially the coastal scenery of Southern England,
cast in the characteristic chalk of the Downs, is taken as a symbol to
represent the country as a whole. In travel posters Beachy Head is raised
to the status of Stonehenge and the Tower of London There are many
miles of magnificent chalk cliffs in eastern and southern England, and
the chalk is perhaps our most impressive cliff builder. The ridges of the
North and South Downs terminate abruptly when they reach the sea
near Folkestone, Dover and Eastbourne respectively. At these points,
and for some distance in both directions along the coast, steep and
often vertical faces form the most familiar cliffed shoreline in the land.
Colour and texture outwardly distinguish them from all other coastal
areas. Altogether this barrier stretching discontinuously from the North
Foreland to the Needles and Lulworth is plainly a shade of white, and
at various points assumes the aspect of a magnificent mural precipice,

17

daubed at the head and foot with the greens of field and sea.

The chalk of Southern England is horizontally bedded (except in the far West) and remarkably compact for so soft a substance. The rock is porous, soluble and crumbly; it collapses readily under pressure and the surface is dry and dusty. In the wet it is extremely slippery – so much so that only nailed boots or boots fitted with crampons will give a non-skid grip. However this kind of footwear tends to grind or break down the holds one might be using so that the precarious adhesion to chalk cannot really be solved. Erosion towards the perpendicular has not been fully explained, but chalk faces in the natural state have a permanently quarried look, as if they had been worked by man. In the West, on the Isle of Wight and in Dorset, a harder chalk lies folded and crushed in a steep plane and is highly resistant to erosion. Here the sea has cut stacks out of the rock which have survived in famous landmarks such as the Needles when entering the Solent and Old Harry on the Channel approach to Poole Harbour.

Beachy Head, forming the East end of the South Downs, is the loftiest headland on the South coast and rises more than 500 ft. above the sea. It is easily the best known chalk cliff in Britain. The pleasure spheres of human interest are such that the Eastbourne fire brigade performs many rescue operations when intrepid holidaymakers get into difficulties by leaving the cliff-top paths. In the middle of the nineteenth century Edward Whymper and his brother clambered on the cliff and nearly broke their necks. Other Victorian mountaineers came to look at the headland and were repulsed if not frightened. Haskett-Smith commented in his *Little Red Book* of 1894 that "the first ascent is made about once in every two years, if we may believe all that we see in the papers". But in 1894 Aleister Crowley, then aged nineteen, made it perfectly clear to the climbing community that Beachy Head was largely a waterworn slope of steep chalk and rotten grass which finished under the commonland in a fringe of cliffs about 150 ft. high. Crowley and his friends climbed the two most conspicuous features on the headland, Etheldreda's Pinnacle and the Devil's Chimney, and boldly attempted other faults in the upper cliffs. One of these called Cuillin Crack, the great fissure on the right side of Etheldreda's, trapped Crowley, and his companion had to summon assistance from the coastguard. These climbs were repeated before the turn of the century; since then there is no record of further

1. Chalk cliffs at Beachy Head, showing the upper wall of 150–200 ft., and the characteristic "slide" terrain of chalk, grass and earth below, at a steep slab-angle down to the beach. Etheldreda's Pinnacle is shown in profile on the far head.

18

authentic ascents. The upper part of Devil's Chimney – a pinnacled mass of rock and not a cleft – has fallen into the sea and is unrecognisable today. Etheldreda's remains intact though somewhat modified in profile when compared with Crowley's photographs. The top is now a platform about 3 ft. square, adorned with a cairn. It is not clear whether this configuration is the work of the pioneers, who freely used ice axes to cut holds in the rock and hack away loose material, or represents the work of later climbers. A party including John Cleare and Tom Patey not long ago tried to repeat the ascent but failed even to reach the access chimneys, called Castor and Pollux by Crowley, below the gap separating the pinnacle from the upper cliff. (Crowley had also climbed the more difficult access chimney on the other – West – side of the gap, by rounding the pillared foot of Etheldreda's Pinnacle). The traverse on a chalk and grass slope of 50° steepness below the cliff proved to be a nightmare of insecurity. One can therefore only marvel at Crowley and his friends who managed to effect a traverse on this slope, up and down, beneath the projections at the cliff-foot in the course of their explorations. Their Grass Traverse, and a shortcut from the top called Etheldreda's Walk – "after a lady who never walked there" – are much more dangerous today. Crowley, subsequently much maligned for his activities in exploring the occult with unnatural and extreme practices of debauchery, summarised the pleasures of Beachy Head climbing as "your reward shall be joy unspeakable in the glorious divinity of sun-glistening altitude and towering whiteness".

Occasionally news of a new direttissima climb on Beachy Head reaches the headlines. In 1971 Mike Taylor, a student of Sussex University, lowered 400 ft. of rope from the telegraph pole on the cliff edge round the corner from Etheldreda's, descended to the bottom and reascended in the line of his rope directly to the top again, using pegs, stirrups and artificial techniques for climbing up a fixed rope, in a total of sixteen hours. Yet for difficulty these cliffs do not compare for a moment with those of half the height which carry on the line westward to Birling Gap and beyond. The tops of these secondary headlands are known as the Seven Sisters. They are mostly vertical and in many places literally overhang the sea. At the foot of them are sea-washed beaches covered with shingle or chalk boulders at low water. At high tide the water laps directly against the sheer cliff faces, cutting off retreat and emphasising the impossible prospect of escape upwards. The most entertaining sea-level traverse

2.   *The inner pinnacle of The Needles on the Isle of Wight, with a tidal race opposing the wind in the gap separating it from the land cliff, seen offshore from an "attack" rubber dinghy.*

hereabouts is to descend from the carpark railings in Birling Gap to the beach, where the cliff is only 30 ft. high and is sometimes accommodated by a periodically repaired iron ladder, and work eastward below the chalk precipices for nearly four miles, past the new lighthouse and round the base of Beachy Head, to where the cliffs relent in the dunes and terraced slopes just before Eastbourne. This traverse requires careful timing in relation to the tide, as a miscalculation in your rate of progress along the awkward beaches by even half an hour may result in the unpleasant task of climbing up and round the shoreline projections near the far end already awash by the incoming tide.

The heroical White Cliffs of Dover are less well-known. In the 1880s A. F. Mummery is reported to have made sea-level traverses on the chalk between Dover and St Margaret's Bay. These take a series of ledges and steps from beach to beach and have been followed several times since. The cliffs in which there are railway cuttings between Folkestone and Dover have also been scaled at various points. A modicum of activity has continued down the years but no modern account of climbing in the vicinity has been published.

Even less has been reported about the continuation chalk beds in the Isle of Wight, which are the thickest in Britain. The complex geology of the island gives rise to many rock formations and correspondingly varied coastal scenery. The vertical folding of chalk is plainly evident on the western tip of the island. On the North side of this promontory, working out of Alum Bay from coloured sandstone structures towards the Needles, and on the South side in Scratchell's Bay, which can only be entered from the sea, ribs of rock rise in a perpendicular plane and alternate with horizontal and angular strata. The cliff in Scratchell's Bay is more imposing than anything on Beachy Head, and parts of the North-side cliff, tinged yellow and orange from sandstones and oxides, resemble Dolomitic walls. The rock is pitted with flints which offer unreliable hold.

Any climbing interest centres on the Needles – three distinctive chalk stacks about 100 ft. high running in a line out to sea, with a lighthouse poised on the base of the outer and tallest one. Strong currents and a tidal race surge through gaps between the stacks, making landing a tricky proposition. The central pinnacle was climbed by Robin Collomb in 1951, using an old clinker rowing boat, on the South face from the inner end, then along the razor edge. In a calm sea it is possible to sail a dinghy under canvas through the gaps, though conditions good enough to achieve this are quite rare (Robin Collomb and Martin Eve, 1965). In normal conditions the only practical and safe procedure is to use a power boat and transfer to a rubber dinghy towed for landing purposes. In 1971 a party of four attempted to make a sea-level traverse from Alum Bay all the way

22

to the Needles. At low water, and after several duckings in the sea, they were stopped about 150 yards short of the target by two caves in the last section of cliff before the promontory. At this point the sea heaves against the cliff all the time. The first assault party of two therefore took to a 7 ft. rubber dinghy and rowed up to the stacks where they were promptly overturned by a huge wave crashing through the first gap. This episode proved the futility of attempting the Needles by any means except from a motor boat anchored at sea.

The Isle of Wight chalk is prolonged as a submarine reef in the Channel opposite Bournemouth. It reappears inland on Ballard Down. The promontory extending from this hill into the sea is the Foreland, which divides the popular bays of Studland and Swanage, just South of Poole Harbour. The tip of this point is composed of razor-edge foreshore stacks, undercut by small caves and tidal channels, and known collectively as Old Harry Rocks. From the furthest stack, out to sea stands Old Harry itself, a slender shining-white pinnacle, one of the most impressive chalk stacks in Britain, and some 70 ft. high. It can only be reached by swimming 40 yards, or from a dinghy, and looks quite unclimbable by any methods known today – with the possible exception of bolting. A successful landing itself would be quite an achievement as a rough sea continuously washes its base. In the narrow channel between Old Harry and the outer razor-edge stands Old Harry's Wife, a dumpy little rock of 25 ft., accessible at normal low water by wading up to the knees in a strong current. Ian Howell climbed it in 1971 and found carved initials on top. The foreshore stacks – surrounded by water at high tide but with a pleasant boulder beach on the North side at low water and joined to the mainland cliff of Ballard Down immediately behind by a narrow wading-channel – were reputed to have been climbed before 1971. However no trace of an ascent of the outer stack was found by the 1971 party, which climbed it and built a cairn facing Old Harry. An attempt on the inner stack failed by 15 ft. due to approaching dusk and an impatient speed-boat driver waiting to take the party off the rocks. The peg for the top-rope descent from this stack was removed by dint of two members at the bottom pulling on it with the rope. (As if to have the last say in the matter the peg hit one of them before landing on the beach.) This climb also showed that an earlier ascent seemed improbable. On these stacks the rock is reasonably good for the first 25–30 ft.; after that it deteriorates rapidly, is very steep and bitty and loosely embedded in earth and vegetation. Large steps have to be cut with short axes and hammers to make safe progress. The rate of climbing on this material is approximately 20 ft. per hour. A few hundred yards further along the cliffs towards Swanage rise another two fine offshore stacks.

Chalk outcrops occur further West along the Dorset coast, where lime-stone cliffs predominate, as far as Lulworth Cove. While it may contribute to spectacular scenery, none of it holds much promise as an acceptable medium for rock climbing. Chalk has already been left alone by several generations of southerners looking for new practice grounds, has been condemned on grounds of safety for just as long, and seems destined to remain the preserve of experimenters. Fore-beach and back-beach traverses, using the slippery cliff above as necessary and according to the movement of tides, may gain some favour as the sea-level traverse along our coastlines is adopted more widely in climbing circles as a recreational pastime. Iron stakes of 10–15 inches, short axes and North-wall type hammers are obligatory equipment. Anyone contemplating a route up-wards could also put to good use a small shovel and even a brush and pan.

Apart from the well known Devonian land-slip which has revealed Middle Chalk along the coast at Beer Head and further east, the only other cliffs in this rock worth mentioning are those composing Flamborough Head in Yorkshire. Up to this point the East Coast consists mainly of slob and salt-marsh. This is the beak of land jutting into the North Sea so well known in classrooms when pupils are asked to draw a map of the country. We have not been able to trace any reference to climbing on this famous headland. The cliffs are exceedingly varied, being pierced with caves and sculpted in huge arches of fantastic shapes, where sea birds breed abun-dantly and have staked a claim to occupation which is unlikely to be disrupted.

3. The stack of Old Harry on the Foreland near Swanage. The climber is standing on Old Harry's Wife. The state of the tide is half an hour before low water.

2   Dorset-Swanage

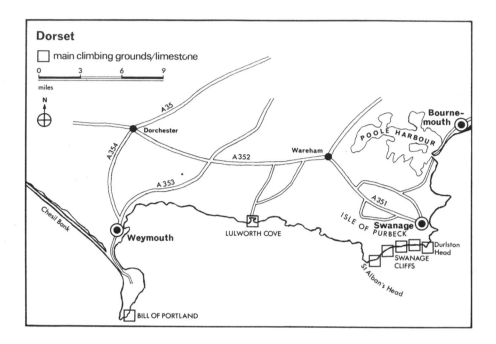

Access: Railway to Swanage. Then on foot or by car in $1\frac{1}{2}$ miles to carpark near Tilly Whim lighthouse. Fee charged in summer for cars. The more westerly cliffs are best reached from Langton Matravers village (bus from Swanage), by motorable lane to Spyway Farm (carpark), then across fields; or by the fair cliff path from lighthouse.

Accommodation: Many hotels and boarding houses in Swanage, unlikely to attract climbers.

Camping: Not permitted in the "lighthouse field" but there are many organised camp sites in the area and friendly farmers whose land borders the cliffs at Langton and Worth Matravers. Numerous "secret places" along the 4 miles of cliff where excellent bivouacs may be had. Take water!

Facilities: General stores at Langton Matravers; town services at Swanage.

Earliest recorded climbs: 1958.

Maps: O.S. One Inch Sheet 179. O.S. $2\frac{1}{2}$ Inch Sheets SY 87/97, SZ 07.

Guidebook: White, R.C., *Dorset*, Climbers' Club, 1969.

26

The five miles of rocky coast between Durlston Head and St Alban's Head west of Swanage are the home of modern sea cliff climbing. Some indication of the momentum gained in this branch of the pastime outside the traditional Cornish playground is revealed by the earliest first ascents in 1958. In under fifteen years Swanage has become a mature and self-prized climbing centre.

The origins of interest in limestone sea cliffs are partially obscure. We know that the development of Swanage owes nothing to inspiration from Cornwall. We know that early visitors put a lot of trust – but not complete faith – in the rock itself, encouraged by experience culled from the Avon Gorge at Bristol (already highly developed by 1960), and to a lesser extent by progress made on the mountain limestone of Derbyshire. The main impetus undoubtedly stems from the search by climbers domiciled in Southern England for "local" practice grounds.

By 1960 the stringent code of mountaineering ethics had disintegrated on the admission and wide acceptance of artificial techniques, coupled with a growing attitude that "anything goes". Liberation from puritanical beliefs – especially in relation to devices designed to safeguard climbers on the rockface and now summed up by the term "protection" – led to an uninhibited hunt for virgin rock all over the country. A cavalier approach to discoveries and a new sort of determination accompanied this enthusiasm, no matter where the cliffs might be situated. In these activities horizons were unlimited. The Swanage cliffs fulfilled the immediate desires of everyone who became seriously associated with them. Most of all the virtues of a maritime setting, with superior and reliable weather, were extolled for their own sake.

Traverses above the sea on the cliffs at Swanage, using natural ledges, provided both the means of examining the limestone in detail and the ideas which led to traversing as an end in itself. The cliffs are composed of an oolitic shelly rock from the uppermost Jurassic beds, known locally as Purbeck Stone and analogous with the neighbouring Portland Stone, a valuable building material. (It is therefore different from the Carboniferous or Mountain Limestone of Derbyshire, Gower and Pembrokeshire, which one associates with the Coal Measures.)

The beds are almost horizontal and rest in massive rectangular blocks jutting out one upon the other a little further, so that the upper tiers often overhang the base. The cliff-top rock is a pronounced yellow and is loose and earthy. However the sea-washed rock is white and almost always sound, and dries with amazing rapidity. In the first 50 ft. of height above the sea the rock retains good frictional properties while slimy conditions between tidal limits on the face are virtually unknown – though the tidal range at Swanage is only 8–10 ft. The scarcity of pronounced

27

features such as buttresses and gullies makes identification of routes from the top nearly impossible. Therefore some sections of the cliffs are committing in that you must descend by abseil towards the sea to examine them, and safety lies at the top of a climb and not at the bottom as in conventional mountaineering.

At Swanage it was soon realised that one must approach the cliffs equipped mentally and materially to deal with the rockface and the sea. A competent sea cliff climber is adept in the generic techniques of cave-swims, pendules, lasso moves and tyroleans. As all sea cliff climbers know, the most dangerous position on a route is at the start at sea-level. Even in a fairly calm sea a huge unexpected wave – traditionally the seventh in a series – can rear up octopus-like and suck a man off a ledge into the hissing cauldron of water. The most frightening part of this experience is a sudden vacuum caused by the wave falling back. The climber, already weakened by the sledge-hammer blow of the wave's arrival, has no air to breathe for a few seconds. It is therefore essential for everyone – climbing or watching – to be well belayed and properly equipped. You cannot lounge in comfort with the contents of a rucksack strewn around out of reach as is the habit on mountain crags.

The Swanage area is of considerable geological interest. The first actual climbers were university geologists on field courses who scrambled at the obvious places where access to the sea via the cliff bottom is easy; places like Dancing Ledges and Tilly Whim and Blackers Hole; many of them in fact are old quarries long since forgotten, where the limestone was loaded directly into boats and where the rusted remains of derricks and even old cannon still stand mute evidence to a once humming industry.

Somehow or other word got round. In the South it was soon realised that limestone was being climbed in the North, and there was a large area of untouched limestone cliff only 100 miles from London. The first serious rock climbs were done in 1958. At first quite independent of each other, two separate groups started to explore the Swanage area and examine its climbing potential.

One of these groups was from Southampton University and their leading light was Barrie Annette, a student reading civil engineering. In fact he moved through the limestone scene like a comet. Experience gained at Swanage from his often solo explorations put him in a strong position when he moved to the more traditional limestone climbing grounds. His zenith perhaps was his first ascent of Unknown Buttress in the Avon Gorge – the "last great problem" for many years at Bristol. At Swanage he was often forced to climb solo through lack of powerful companions. It took a long time to live down an epic which occurred during one of his early attempts at the obvious line which was to become Marmolata. He was benighted, possibly intentionally, at the cliff bottom, a place reached easily only by abseil, and settled down to a comfortable and well-equipped bivouac. His failure to return for a date led to questions at the police station. Eventually Barrie was forcibly rescued by the Swanage lifeboat after a night-search operation. The first of many subsequently similar questions were raised in the local paper about mad-fool climbers, though how were they to know that he was as much in control of the situation on a ledge above the waves as when sitting in the lecture theatre.

The other group belonged to no particular club but were all alpinists of considerable experience, who lived in the London or Guildford areas: Gunn Clark, Peter Bell, Tony Smythe, John Cleare and their friends. They soon met up with the Southampton group and much exploration was shared in the early days. Development was concentrated at first near those easy ways down, especially at the East (Tilly Whim) end of the cliffs. The Subluminal Cliff, just below the lighthouse, was soon worked out. It gave vertical one-pitch climbs of all technical grades to VI, starting from a broad traverse ledge just above the sea. This cliff was particularly attractive because the pioneers were frightened by the tops of the higher cliffs, where the rock, already loosening, gave way to vertical earth studded with shaky flakes before becoming steep grass. Worse still, there were no finishing belays. This of course is common to nearly all limestone cliffs, especially sea cliffs, but Subluminal finishes with a safe mantelshelf on to almost flat limestone pavé. Here one could learn just what was and what wasn't possible on Swanage rock.

The next cliff zone to be developed was the Tilly Whim Caves, an old quarry. This section lies within the Durlston Castle Estate, private property, and normal access is through a turnstile and down a "smugglers' passage" carved in the rock. The Southampton climbers worked on the short free routes between the old quarry floor and the sea, while Smythe and Cleare put up peg routes on the smooth 70 ft. walls above. Perhaps the best lines were Poem Wall, taking a thin crack through a smooth wall on which is carved "Prospero's Farewell" – done in February 1960 and Poem Corner, an adjoining dièdre, a bold free line led by Ian Mc-Morrin. A little later ownership changed hands at Durlston Castle. A steel fence barred the 10 ft. "Diff." which gave access to the Caves, and climbing is now forbidden in the main area. In the other parts of the Tilly Whim Cliffs parties may climb only in the winter months and then only with permission from the Castle office – a privilege likely to be withdrawn.

A descent from the eastern end of the Caves leads to an area, still governed by the Castle edict, where there are several fantastic routes which fell at an early date, mainly because it seemed that the finishes were up natural features and might therefore be relatively safe. Rendez-

4.   *The classic route of Rendezvous Manqué on the Tilly Whim cliffs at Swanage.*

vous Manqué, opened by Clark and Smythe, is an improbable line, only IV+, which seems to peter out below overhangs. The route dives into a cave, deep in the bowels of the cliff, and chimneys its way up to reappear in the light of an upper chimney. From here a bit of back-and-foot work leads to the grassy clifftop and the tourist path. One leader, bringing up his "invisible" second and "playing" the rope, once claimed to a puzzled tripper that he was shark fishing. A bobbing lobster float visible through a slight dip in the cliff added to the story.

Steeple Groove is another sensational route. An obvious dièdre is gained by swinging out along a small roof on good jugs and a straight two-hand pull-up. Again there is an excellent finish to the climb. The first ascent was probably by Peter Bell.

In the autumn of 1963 a development took place which started a new trend in the thinking of sea cliff climbing. Rusty Baillie, fresh from his success with Haston on the Eigerwand, and John Cleare drove a line horizontally from Tilly Whim to Subluminal, a distance of some 250 yards on the map, through an area still virgin and where the cliff bottomed in deep water. Traverse of the Gods was the result. It is a route involving nearly 2,000 ft. of climbing and scrambling, various rope-moves and a short swim. It was the first of the modern sea traverses and paved the way for the future when the same team got the traversing notion underway in Torbay with Magical Mystery Tour. They were, after all, only treating these low cliffs as an Alpine problem, and linking two easy ways down to the sea by the easiest line. The natural line on so many sea cliffs just happens to be horizontal. Of course, this is due to the horizontal bedding of the strata.

At Swanage there is a geological phenomena known as the Puffin Fault. This is an horizontal band which runs for miles through the lime-stone, from its first outcropping at Durlston Head, west towards St Alban's Head. Sometimes it dips below the sea, sometimes it forms the base of great roofs or caves, sometimes it forms ledges as at Subluminal, and sometimes just a naturally eroded fingery crack half way up the cliffs. Traverse of the Gods follows this line much of the way; and on the far side of the Subluminal section, Nutcracker takes the same fault to the next cliff section where, above large boulders in the sea, several slightly longer routes lead back to the clifftop. These go at about Grade III or IV and soon after this we reach the Boulder Ruckle, possibly the most serious stretch of developed sea-cliff climbing in Southern England.

The Ruckle is a straight line of South-facing cliffs, some 900 yards long, always over 110 ft. high, lacking in prominent features, always vertical and often overhanging, and bottoming in a narrow line of huge boulders against which the sea pounds and surges. The way along the bottom,

31

among the boulders, is a scramble, but at either end escape is blocked by difficult ground. The traverse East to the Nutcracker Exit and Subluminal is long; unless the tide is low and the sea calm it will entail a wade. Although it is technically the easiest way out of the Ruckle, experienced parties have had to fight for their lives on this section in bad weather or in the dark. The exit West towards the Cattle Troughs by Paradise Street is more difficult, though only Grade IV in the reverse direction. From the last boulders of the Ruckle it involves a fingery climb up an overhanging wall at Grade VI to reach the Puffin Fault.

Near the western end, Boulder Ruckle Exit is the usual way out. A scramble up a peculiar ramp across a blank wall leads to within 20 ft. of the clifftop grass. Cleare, Smythe and Clark, who made the first ascent in the late 1950s, were compelled to climb this last section artificially. They found that pegs placed between the loose blocks were more predictable than the loose blocks themselves. Ten years of gardening removed most of the loose material and the Exit is now graded IV. A party new to the area would do well to enter the Ruckle by this route and to leave a rope in place on this upper section. The top is difficult to find on the featureless grassland above but the 8th fence post east of the 2nd stile west of the lighthouse is the abseil point. It is usual to use several of the posts and as many bushes as possible to safeguard the anchorage. It is only 60 ft. down from this point to the top of the ramp.

Another feasible entry is a 120 ft. free abseil down Marmolata itself – the only real future of the Ruckle and easily identified looking West from the lighthouse area. Marmolata is one of the Swanage classics, and was climbed at an early date. Clark and Cleare were first to the top, but they were benighted and used a rope from above on the last section. Later Clark climbed it clean with J. Histed. The finish was across the right wall of the great dièdre/chimney, and this is still loose and has lost many of the features of the first ascent. A pleasanter line aesthetically is to take the lower overhanging flake chimney, once graded A2, now climbed free (VI, strenuous), then a second pitch follows the Puffin Fault out left to a ledge on the crest of the buttress. Here the line of Tatra – an Annette route – joins from the left, and two more short pitches lead by difficult but well protected cracks and excellent rock to a solid finish.

There are routes every few yards now along Boulder Ruckle, but none of them is easy. They are all serious and many of the finishes are not very solid. To the experienced limestone climber the Ruckle will give great

5.   Traverse of the Gods; climbers working along the first pitch towards a cave. Note the discontinuous ledge formation just above the sea which gives the route.

sport, but the novice should learn his craft elsewhere – there are still several miles to go to St Alban's Head.

Cattle Troughs is the next area, a series of amphitheatres and sea-level ledges which give access to many easier and popular climbs on good rock up to 50 ft. in height; and the Promenade, an area of slightly longer climbs, which leads to Fisherman's Ledge. Here are several big roofs with peg routes over them and some hard lines of 70–80 ft. Finally, a huge cave of deep water bars the way West and an exit can be made, past a rusty chain and iron spike to the clifftop. There are various lines but the easiest is a magnificent scramble called Helix (II).

A fine expedition for a powerful and fit party is the traverse of one and a quarter miles as the crow flies from Tilly Whim to Fisherman's Ledge, joining up Traverse of the Gods, Paradise Street, and the interesting connecting walls and zawns between Cattle Troughs, the Promenade and Fisherman's Ledge. The time for a fast team of two would be five hours.

Further West along the coast there are many other areas for climbing. Some have been explored, such as Blackers Hole, an old quarry with good peg and free routes where climbing is possible in the worst sea conditions. Guillemot Ledges, a short section of Boulder Ruckle-type cliff just East of Dancing Ledges, gives excellent routes with a sound finish on quarried pavement at the clifftop. Dancing Ledges, a tourist venue, has many short problems. At Seacombe and Whinspit there are more old quarries, leading finally to St Alban's Head, where the limestone climbs slowly away from the sea and the crags fall into thick jungly undercliff. The rock here is very loose but there are rough-sea routes of up to 80 ft.

Rescue on the Swanage cliffs is not easy and more harm may be done to a victim by the sea than results from a fall. There have been several drowning accidents. Under ideal conditions evacuation is possible with an inflatable rescue dinghy, then straight into the lifeboat, but usually the coastguards have to do a clifftop haul. In case of an accident the Tilly Whim lighthouse is the key to all further assistance. Relations with the local authorities are less than good. Cases of vandalism have been blamed on climbers and there have been accidents to children, unruly youths and tourists who have been trying to emulate the real climbers they see. In the future it is up to climbers to make certain that things go well and not worse so that climbing is not banned on this wonderful section of cliff. In any case the cliffs are all on private property.

6.   An end-on view of Boulder Ruckle at Swanage, showing the intimidating sea wall rising directly from the boulder beach. Peter Biven prospecting a new route.

West of St Alban's Head the limestone disappears. The coast becomes a succession of muddy shales and high and impressive chalk bastions reaching up to 500 ft. In two places, however, the harder rock returns, briefly at Lulworth and more solidly on the Isle of Portland, which is composed entirely of excellent limestone.

Lulworth Cove is a prime day-tripper resort. There are huge car and coach parks and rows of ice cream and candy floss stalls. The beach of the quaint cove may be thick with tourists but out on the headlands of the cove the scenery changes. The actual coast hereabouts is a thin band of limestone through which the sea has broken at one point to carve out the unique circular cove in the softer chalk behind. The jaws of the cove – the twin headlands – are made of limestone. Several routes have been put up on the western headland, and round the corner, at Stair Hole, and a little way to the West at the interesting natural arch of Durdle Door. These are rather scrappy and very loose climbs, and the coastguard, who have a watch-house on top of the headland, do not take kindly to climbers. The notices in Lulworth forbidding climbing are so numerous that it would seem that the locals have a phobia about it. The trouble is that small boys have to be rescued on most days in the summer from the easy-angled chalk cliffs that surround the cove.

On going round the corner of the eastern headland all sight and sound of the hordes are lost. The cliffs form a wall bottoming in the sea and are capped with large chalky overhangs; they stretch thus for a mile to Mupe Bay. The traverse of this wall, from Lulworth to the Mupe Rocks stacks, is a first-class expedition, and is technically not difficult. It is fairly serious however, because a mile is a long way and only in one section, some 200 yards from the start, is escape possible upwards, at the Fossil Forest. Should this be chosen the climber then lands himself in the middle of the Army's Lulworth tank range, closed to the public and full of unexploded missiles! The higher the tide, the more difficult the rock that one is obliged to climb. At low tide with a calm sea much of the traverse is a scramble along easy ledges, dodging the waves. In heavy weather the traverse is very serious indeed. The final section before Mupe Stacks involves a climb at about Grade III for some 60 ft. up the wall to large ledges which lead down into Mupe Bay. This climb bypasses an unclimbable overhung section and a deep zawn. There is scope for several full-sized upward routes at this end of the cliffs. The limestone now peters out into a line of stacks and skerries. Mupe Bay gives excellent bathing although sometimes

7. Ian Howell leading Bottomless Buttress on the Boulder Ruckle cliff at Swanage.

swimmers find the remains of old shells in the water. The route back to Lulworth is by a well marked path through the Range. This is difficult to locate, intentionally, from the other direction.

At Portland the climbs are rather disappointing. Many of them are short but technical difficulties reach the highest grades. The Isle has been developed almost exclusively by a resident, the Rev. R. L. M. Shepton.

8. Part of the Lulworth-Mupe Bay sea level traverse, shot at low water and revealing the easier traversing prospects in this condition.

3 South Devon

Access: Railway to Torbay resorts. All the main cliffs lie within the borough resorts. Normally cars can be taken to within 100–200 yards of the cliff-tops. Certain cliffs require written permission (permits) from the local authority, and the Old Redoubt cliff is out of bounds during the nesting season from Easter to July.

Accommodation: Hotels and boarding houses by the score.

Camping: Sleeping on the cliff tops is forbidden (and much too public to be practical). There are numerous official campsites in and around the Torbay resorts.

Facilities: Services of every description are generally available within one mile of all the cliffs.

Earliest recorded climbs: 1961.

Introductory classics: Love Not War (Babbacombe), The Gates of Eden (Daddyhole), Moonraker (Old Redoubt).

Maps: O.S. One Inch, Sheet 188. O.S. $2\frac{1}{2}$ Inch, Sheets SX 85/95, SX 86/96.

Guidebook: Littlejohn, P.R., and Biven, P.H., *South Devon Climbers' Guide*, West Col Productions, 1971.

Climbing on sea cliffs in south Devon is centred within and on either side of Torbay. Exploration has been an extension by a separate group of climbers of the ideas that realised the potential of the Swanage area. Torbay is a deep bite in the coast, facing east; the name is synonymous with the resorts of Torquay, Paignton and Brixham. Two claw-like promontories to the North and South, Hope's Nose and Berry Head, enclose the bay; fashionable suburbs of Torquay and Brixham respectively encroach on these headlands while Paignton spreads along the back of the bay. The Devonian Limestone of the region is a grey rock, older than the material at Swanage. Much of it has been quarried so that smooth and massive limestone sheets of picturesque but unfriendly aspect rule the scene. The pristine rock falling straight into the sea is darker and fairly clean and is riddled with grottoes and potholes. Consequently nearly all

9. (overleaf) Peter Biven negotiating the crux section of the Magical Mystery Tour traverse on the Old Redoubt cliff, Berry Head.

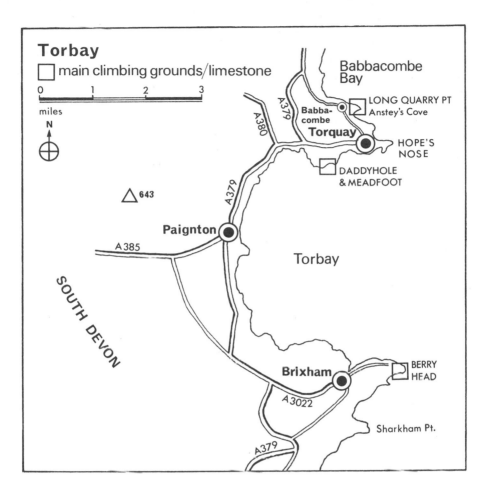

the coastline worthy of attention, notwithstanding the complications of natural erosion, was traversed piece by piece at sea-level before the best lines to the top of particular cliffs were worked out. The traverse under the Old Redoubt cliff beyond Berry Head, called Magical Mystery Tour, is recorded in its technical description as 7,700 ft., an unprecedented length in British rock climbing and daunting even by Alpine standards. Any kind of climbing on these cliffs is just about the newest for a coastal area that can already be regarded as developed. Apart from a dilettante inspection of Berry Head in the early sixties, nothing of note appears in the emerging annals of South Devon sea cliff climbing until 1967.

The percipient mountaineering figure of the Exeter region is Peter Biven. He has a curious place in the exploration of practice cliffs, in having previously built a reputation as a developer of postwar Derbyshire gritstone and limestone and then faded – it was thought – without trace. In the North it was believed that he had enjoyed a period of rejuvenation in the company of his constant companion, Trevor Peck (who was genuinely approaching middle age). When no more news of their activity was forthcoming it was assumed he had "retired". One of the best stories of this period – there are several versions of it – so characteristic of the image created by the Biven-Peck team, was of the pair driving along jeep roads over forbidden moors in a Rolls-Royce, up to the foot of forbidden crags, and making forbidden climbs with equanimity while gamekeepers opened and closed gates for them and doffed their hats in salute. As Eric Byne has recorded in *High Peak*, Biven was twenty years old and Peck about fifty when they climbed the famous Moyer's Buttress at Gardom's Edge in 1955. This story and many others we hear about Biven and Peck are substantially true.

In the early years of Biven's residence in Exeter he concentrated with Peck and others on expanding the playground of Cornish granite. Inland crags of Devon and Lundy also received his attention. Indeed these were the sole areas of activity for all climbers in the South-West. During the early sixties Biven and others had examined some of the cliffs in Torbay and came away unimpressed. Visitors to Exeter, who, if they were of the right calibre, were put up in a spare bed or on the floor in the Biven household, were taken usually to Chudleigh Rocks for a taste of South Devon limestone. There they were perhaps shown round not too carefully to ensure that the Biven-Cannings-Littlejohn syndicate and the Exeter group did not lose any important first ascents. In the evening you could rely on a good dinner and become engaged in polemic discussion with Peter's attractive wife, Polly, as to the moral state of the nation, why climbers are bad at most things except climbing, and how youth today should not be deterred from taking advantage of an enlightened society because earlier conventions and restraints had robbed an older generation of growing up too quickly. The course of the debate may not be entirely consistent with the views one might conservatively expect from the spouse of a J.P. A stranger could be forgiven for thinking that his intrusion was welcomed except on the crags. Conversely the climbing movement in the South-West had never been taken seriously by the forces operating in the North. Frank Cannings, one of the most persistent and successful leaders of the Exeter group, was denigrated by pundits of Craig Gogarth after his critical appraisal of development on that Anglesey sea cliff merely because he worked in a backwater of the modern movement. When part of the Anglesey television team spectacular was invited to Berry Head to

10. Climbers ascending Moonraker on the Old Redoubt cliff at Berry Head.

examine the cliffs for a possible national broadcast, a decision was post-poned for future consideration. The intrinsic merits of a sea cliff cannot be translated in terms of a mountain crag and comparison is futile. These merits were missed just as Biven and others had missed them originally. The criteria posed by Gogarth paradoxically rest entirely within the landcliff idiom. On Anglesey the sea was ignored at first, then its presence was acknowledged as a nuisance, and finally climbers were forced to come to terms with it as the space to manoeuvre on new rock grew more restricted. Mainstream exploration of mountain cliffs has only influenced coastal development in so far as conventional techniques can be applied. In Torbay, and more so at Swanage, new skills had to be perfected to move along the waterline mindful entirely of the sea and its tidal variations.

It is quite unique that a new branch of the mountaineering pastime should have had one of its important development stages conducted amid a background of notable seaside resorts – from high-flown Torquay, the Monte Carlo of the South Coast, to more knock-about Brixham with its fishing fleet. Until about 1965 sea cliffs had been treated as land cliffs that bottomed in water instead of scree and grass. It is natural to walk along the top of a sea cliff – an age-old pastime, and in climbing it is equally natural to look for a way along the bottom. At the turn of the century A. W. Andrews advocated coastal traverses but the possibilities he saw in Cornwall were not taken up seriously. A similarly unreceptive situation clouds the exploratory work of C. H. Archer in North Devon (see Chapter 6). In the early sixties he stirred even less interest than Andrews over half a century ago.

The difference between these tentative ideas and the serious sea cliff traverse is one of degree. The originators used the foreshore as tides allowed, scrambling from beach to beach, and occasionally climbed on to the rockface, assuming it to be possible, when the sea left no room to manoeuvre below. The challenge of including the passage of a cliff at high water, with or without a foreshore, belonged to the realm of rock climbing.

So many problems are encountered in pursuing the cliff traverse that the job has to be approached in the manner of an expedition, like an alpine climb, instead of a practice cliff route. While the weather may govern all kinds of climbing to some extent, the sea traverse is further complicated by the condition of the sea, and techniques more nautical than land-based have to be introduced. Wet suits as used for skin-diving were brought into the Torbay scene. Loaded with gear the climber had to make swimming pitches, the rope trailing behind in the sea, and use new lasso techniques to arrange protection from the rocks above as he went along. Some of the special problems include judging distances, downward pegging round blind projections, working in the sea with a lot of equipment, and estimating the occurrence of sea-filled obstacles like caves, zawns and blowholes which can rarely be seen till the last moment. Inspection of sea cliffs from a distance is even less profitable than the old game of picking out features on a mountain from across the valley. Biven has devised a method of personal buoyancy for the non-swimming climber. This consists of putting the contents of a rucksack into a polythene bag, replacing it in the sack and inflating the bag. The rucksack can then be put on back to front and is secured to the climber's chest by tying the shoulder straps together at the back. After tying on the rope he can now, in the author's own words, "hurl himself clear of the rocks . . . and is virtually unsinkable". Techniques have been developed for working with a small rubber dinghy fitted with a thin nylon painter up to 100 ft. long. Some cliffs and stacks can only be reached conveniently from the sea. You have to know whether it is possible to land directly off a wooden or glass-fibre boat, or if transfer to a smaller rubber dinghy is necessary; where anchor lines can be attached to hold against current and tide; and the method of ferrying equipment on to the rockface. The logistics of serious sea cliff climbing are enormous by ordinary mountain standards. You may also be faced with moving some or all equipment constantly along the cliff up to three times the normal in bulk and weight. A small miscalculation in the nautical requirements of the expedition can result in failure to start a climb, and poor seamanship can lead to the loss of valuable equipment.

No one worries unduly about getting saturated in salt water while fully clothed, though this condition does not improve the life of expensive hardware. Everyone aims to avoid it as far as possible. However, to combat the special discomforts that arise many liberties alien to the ethics of modern rock climbing have been taken during the genesis of coastal exploration. The time cannot be far away when a code of fair play will be formulated. Rough and unpredictable seas invariably hasten the application of excessive aid and protective measures. A scale of values according to prevailing conditions seems desirable, even though the mountaineering community as a whole dissents from this as a practice and frequently condemns transgressors. (A simple example would be to grade a rock pitch either as VI, or with artificial aid, V and A1, leaving the choice to the climber.) A large amount of difficult horizontal movement is axiomatic in sea traverses. On land crags and mountains it was shown long ago that similar movement requires precautions different from those needed for moving up and down a rockface. Add to the proposition bird-droppings, seaweed, and angry sea and violent waves, then the problems of safety pass through the filters of change and the actions of climbers are distorted beyond recognition. The evidence that all sea cliff climbing is serious and needs an ethical and material technique of its own is reinforced by the fact that all recent deaths in the South have been due to drowning.

The potential for traversing in the Torbay area was first demonstrated by Rusty Baillie and John Cleare. They had previously set a similar example at Swanage in Traverse of the Gods. On New Year's Eve, 1967 they completed the waterline girdle of the Old Redoubt cliff when the rock was cold and clammy but the sea temperature was much higher. The traverse was called Magical Mystery Tour (VI). This became the first of four continuation traverses, extending in total for nearly 1½ miles. Peter Biven quickly grasped the significance of the Baillie/Cleare expedition, and many miles of traverses were produced by him in the next two years.

The Old Redoubt became the most important single cliff in Torbay after Biven and Littlejohn made the first route to the top of it in August, 1967. This was Moonraker (250 ft., VI). By the end of the year Biven had been joined by Frank Cannings who led the magnificent and ferocious Barbican (320 ft., VI+), and the two climbers also made Pikadon. These climbs compared favourably with the toughest lines emerging on Anglesey. Meanwhile the full-scale exploration of other cliffs had begun.

About half a mile along the clifftop from the Imperial Hotel in Torquay steep scrambles and slides in thorns and on shale can be made into Daddyhole Cove. This rocky inlet with a tidal boulder beach has a main cliff and two secondary ones, while another quarried face stands above Triangle Point on the east side. These cliffs are now combed by many routes, and the cove can be entered from either side at sea-level by the Plimsoll Line or Pinnacle Traverse, both classic, entertaining and not really difficult. Continuation traverses to the West are in a different class; the last section, with the provocative name of Five Star Traverse, creeps surreptitiously across the low cliff under the garden and grounds of the swanky Imperial before petering out below the Marine Spa Ballroom. In the Daddyhole area all climbing has now been "regularised". Previously, sea cliff explorers were liable to be chased by council officials and workmen, till the climbers got onto the cliffs where they were unapproachable. Because beach-dwellers might be struck by falling rock, or stray on to the cliffs themselves out of curiosity, the Exeter group made their peace with the Torbay resorts and agreed to abide by a system of permits, which are now issued on application to bonafide parties.

The Daddyhole Main Cliff is generally excellent rock and the foot of the face is unaffected by tides. Corners and grooves in the steep wall supply most of the lines, up to 180 ft. high. The classic route is The Gates of Eden (V−), and equally good or better at a higher standard are Gargantua

11.   *Daddyhole Main Cliff, on the outskirts of Torquay, seen from Triangle Point. Sea-level traverses of considerable interest enter and leave the boulder-filled cove at its foot.*

(VI), Triton (VI−), Fandangle (VI−) and The Pearl (V). The upper cliffs in the cove are at present looser and dirty and more difficult of access through natural obstacles. The nature of routes here is reflected in names like Loose Knickers and Ramshackle. The East retaining parapet of Meadfoot Quarry resembles more the Main Cliff in quality, but with shorter climbs and greater exposure to the tourist hordes. About half a dozen members of the Exeter group concentrated on the Daddyhole area in 1967 and produced the majority of routes in under two years.

East of Meadfoot Sands we soon reach the northern extremity of Torbay at Hope's Nose. The other area of major development lies round this corner, in Anstey's Cove and on the quarried plateau of its enclosing promontory, called Long Quarry Point. This is fringed with a fine if somewhat small series of pinnacles which in places are disposed to re- semble an Alpine ridge. This feature of the Point provided the original attraction to climbers. They soon went away, having ignored the huge quarried faces above and the adjoining rock buttresses on either side, and did not return for five years. Subsequent climbing on these cliffs is more serious than Daddyhole, certainly longer, and has a style of its own distinct from the Berry Head-Old Redoubt faces. Most of them are well clear of tidal starts, while the sea traverses from Anstey's Cove towards the Point, called the Long Traverse, and its counterpart round the other side under Babbacombe Crags, called The Kraken, are separate entities. The Long Traverse (IV to V+, according to tactics and direction taken) was made as far back as 1962. It is one of Biven's party pieces when visitors are brought to Long Quarry Point for the first time. Halfway along you arrive at an alarming gash in the cliff known as the Sanctuary. Its con- tinuation wall has serious routes of its own. As when Biven is sitting on the Bench, so here, in conditions of high water, the options of traversing are politely explained to the ruffled newcomer. You can either climb round the rock chamber with considerable difficulty and be prepared to fall off into the sea or elect for the resigned gesture of swimming to the other side. If the second course is adopted, someone will almost certainly utter the discouraging remark, "chicken". Biven contends that there is a proper time and place for swimming tactics in sea traverses. For example, when he and Cannings swam in from the sea to the foot of a cliff on Little Orme in North Wales, it was to demonstrate to a rival party trying to descend the cliff on a rope from the top that superior approach methods perfected in the South could gain the upper hand. But once you had found

12. Crossing the Sanctuary on the Long Traverse from Anstey's Cove out to Long Quarry Point near Torquay.

a way on to the face, for moving across or climbing up it, the main object is to remain in contact with the rock, and not to avoid particular difficulties by taking to water again as a matter of course.

The back walls of Long Quarry Point are the special preserve of Pat Littlejohn. There are quarried and natural faces of continuous steepness, which a few years ago would have repelled all climbers. The average route is of 250 ft., often on doubtful rock though several can now be declared sound. A representative selection would include Steppenwolf (VI), Grip Type Thynne (VI) and Magic Carpet Ride (VI−). Shorter routes on the large outcrops in Anstey's Cove offer alternative easier climbing, some distance above the sea and usually with an audience of peddle boats. The best known of these is Saint Gregory the Wonder Worker (180 ft., IV+). On the North side of Long Quarry Point the waterline approaches to Babbacombe Crags are quite secluded, for they are guarded either end by the Kraken Traverse. At the Long Quarry Point end the cliffs are marked by the imposing Love Not War buttress (250 ft., IV−), an excellent introductory climb starting a few feet above the waves, and with rock in parts doubtful enough to dispel casual attitudes that might be imported from the mountains.

By 1970 the indomitable trio of Biven Cannings and Littlejohn had transformed the face of the Old Redoubt cliff into a snakes and ladders board. Among the best of the more recent routes are the Goddess of Gloom (230 ft., VI) and Dreadnought (310 ft., VI+). Round the headland on Berry Head Quarry a climb called Yellow Rurties (170 ft., VI) has put this cliff firmly on the hard man's map. Some of the climbing on Berry Head has become almost too close for comfort and recalls again the overcrowded rockfaces of British mountains. The effects of rock starvation felt by those who are continually trying to open up new areas of interest along our coastlines are accelerating activity beyond previous rates of progress in British climbing annals. It has taken only three years of − admittedly − intense exploration to work up Torbay from almost total obscurity to one of the most important regional sea cliff climbing locations in the country. One foresees increasing animosity arising between growing bands of climbers drifting into seaside areas and the more orderly regimented masses of people who staked their claim to such places nearly a century ago.

13. Peter Biven attempting a Grade VI route on the sea face of Quarry Pinnacle at Long Quarry Point.

14. (next page) The Slabs at Long Quarry Point. Frank Cannings leading the second ascent of Grip Type Thynne.

4 Cornwall

Access: Railway to St Ives and Penzance. Frequent bus services by Western National to Sennen, Land's End, Porthcurno, St Just, Bosigran, etc.

Accommodation: Bosigran Count House, private property owned by the Climbers' Club. Farmhouse and inn/hotel accommodation in all parts of West Penwith.

Camping: By private arrangement with a limited number of farmhouses. Indiscriminate camping is generally forbidden, especially on National Trust land.

Facilities: Shops and main services in most villages. Earliest recorded climbs: 1902 (scrambles dating back to 1858).

Maps: O.S. One Inch, Sheet 189, O.S. $2\frac{1}{2}$ Inch, Sheets SW 43, 33, 32.

Climbing guidebook: Biven, P. H., McDermott, , Stevenson, V, *Cornwall*, Climbers' Club, 2 vols., 1966, 1968.

Cornwall is too well known and for the most part overcrowded in summer to warrant detailed description. Though not favoured with an exceptional climate (the annual rainfall is greater than London) the coast fairly deserves the name of the English Riviera. Like its more famous counterpart it is as equally varied. Within a few miles the land tilts gently into the sea through sheltered bays and wooded estuaries, or falls suddenly in one step from a prickly gorse moor down to waves pounding against a bare rockface. Busy holiday haunts are squeezed at intervals into coves while the longer stretches of cliff between them are comparatively deserted.

Of the two peninsulas forming an arched foot dipping its big toe into the grey Atlantic the northerly one displays the finest rock scenery. The toe is known as West Penwith. From Hayle and Marazion two roads skirting the moor of West Penwith to reach Land's End take you into a world remote even from the fascinating strangeness that Cornwall exercises in general over the visitor. It is a world with a few pockets of picturesque maritime habitations, like the small fishing communities of St Ives, Newlyn and Mousehole, and of strands speckled with sun-seekers as at Whitesand Bay, Sennen and Lamorna. Outside of these the coast on both sides of Land's End is girdled by a belt of granite cliffs with one of the most complex topographical plans in Britain. The hinterland is strewn with prehistoric earthworks, standing stones and

circles (called Hurlers) and derelict holy wells. The local rocking stones are called Logan rocks. This wealth of Megalithic monuments is not always easily identified because old and extensive mining operations have destroyed some of it, and luxuriant vegetation has overgrown other sites. Deserted tin mines, their chimneys and engine houses are familiar Cornish landmarks. The early settlements and old language are now mystical in the county's history; exploring the remains does not appear to be one of the major attractions to visitors. In 1337 Cornwall was created a duchy for the Black Prince. Since this time the eldest son of the sovereign has been Duke of Cornwall and it is the oldest dukedom in the kingdom.

The Royal Duchy has a special place in sea cliff climbing. It was here that it all started. At the turn of the last century a young man who was active in the exploration of Snowdonia revisited his uncle's home in West Penwith where he had spent boyhood holidays. He was now able to appreciate the magnificence of the wild, rock-bound coastline, and was probably aware that references to climbing in Cornwall had already appeared in print. So that in 1902 when A. W. Andrews embarked in earnest on his solitary quest it was in the spirit of established attitudes and rules adopted in mountaineering at that time. Yet almost immediately he saw the possibility of horizontal climbing – the sea-level traverse. This was slowly to dictate the course and trends that modern sea cliff climbing took, and was to become one of the main differences involving new techniques between coastal and inland cragsmanship. However, Cornwall as the earliest coastal region to be developed in Britain, and the only one acknowledged to exist before the Second World War, grew up in the tradition of the inland crag on British mountains; moreover as a poor relation. It remained so until the middle of the 1950s. The first guidebook for climbers, issued in 1950, had an almost apologetic tone for describing the granite cliffs in detail, and in fact half the volume was devoted to walking on the moors.

Having reached a certain maturity, it now seems that modern sea cliff climbing has become a separate branch of the pastime which did not evolve from the progressive activities begun in Cornwall. There are two fundamental reasons for believing this. Firstly, the late adoption of limestone as an acceptable climbing material. Supposedly loose, and quite different from granite, this rock demands new fields of experience and technique to achieve the same degree of safety and confidence. Experiments with limestone climbing on a national scale had begun seriously in the Derbyshire Peak District only in the fifties. The lessons of this

15.   (previous page) The upper part of the Bosigran Ridge gives excellent practice for climbers to move together as in Alpine climbing.

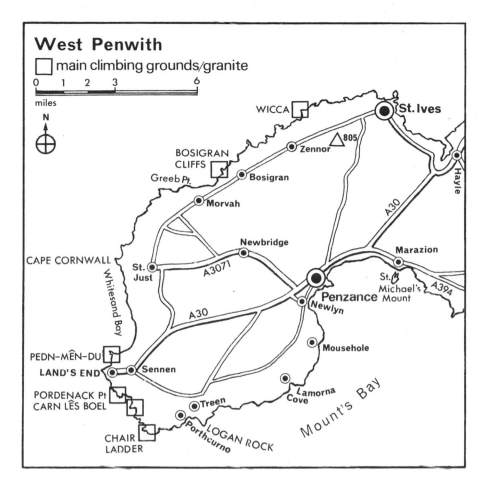

West Penwith

☐ main climbing grounds/granite

0   1   2   3   6

miles

N

WICCA ☐   ● **St. Ives**

● Zennor   △ 805

BOSIGRAN CLIFFS

Greeb Pt.   ● **Bosigran**

● **Morvah**

Newbridge ●

Marazion ●

CAPE CORNWALL

St. ● **Just**   A3071

Whitesand Bay

A30

● Penzance St.   Michael's   Mount

● Newlyn

A394

A30

● **Mousehole**

PEDN–MÊN–DU ☐

LAND'S END ●   ● **Sennen**

PORDENACK Pt
CARN LÊS BOEL

● **Treen**

● Lamorna Cove

Mount's Bay

CHAIR LADDER ☐

Porthcurno   LOGAN ROCK

experience were carried almost immediately to long and hitherto untouched stretches of our limestone seaboards where the development of new techniques occurred. The potential of sea cliffs was realised by those living near them, as the gritstone had been long ago, but only after faith in the rock had been established. Secondly, it became *à la mode* in new sea cliff locations to persevere with the traverse-type of route. Up-and-down climbs could either be impossible, too difficult or dangerous because of steep grass, earth and vegetation, sometimes too short to be worthwhile, or because by emerging at the top you could be trespassing in someone's garden and were in danger of being bitten by the dog. Near sea-level and for thirty or forty feet above the waves the rock is usually firm. Though Andrews might have wished otherwise, the great sea traverses of Britain are found outside Cornwall. The route to the top of the cliff on sound granite all the way predominates. The position is made clear in the latest guidebook to West Penwith: "A good deal of space in the 1950 guidebook was devoted to the traverses below high water mark originated by A. W. Andrews. These are no longer in fashion so have been omitted."

Most climbers visiting Cornwall since the popular invasion started in the fifties are seeking the climbing they are accustomed to in North Wales and the Lake District, with the additional promise of fine weather. The alien element of sea and coastal surroundings is gratuitous, and visitors quickly adapt to it – sometimes to the point of preference. In terms of scale the Cornish cliffs lie midway between large crags on our high mountains and outcrops of the Midlands and North. In nature they are unlike either and the rock is not bettered anywhere in the country. Cornish granite gives a delicate, friction-style climbing using tiny quartz crystals on its slabs and walls, or very strenuous work with painful handjams and pull-ups in its rock faults. There are lots of good cracks for strong fingers, and difficulty is directly related to the steepness of a face. Over geological years the wind and seas of Atlantic gales have eroded the cliffs into a multitude of features. Among these the zawn is prominent, either as a way down as in a gully to the sea where climbs can be started, or when steep-sided and full of water at low tide as a formidable barrier when attempting to traverse at sea-level for any distance. In any case all movements at sea-level are conditioned by the state of the tide and the movement of water. Most of the recent hard new routes are on the zawn walls, where the rock is usually vertical or overhanging, and these walls can now be seen to be among the highest cliffs on the granite littoral. Flying buttresses between these zawns and other rocky inlets provide pinnacled ridges similar to those on high mountains, and of several hundred feet in length. Not all the cliffs bottom in water, and access along grassy rakes and, at high tide, wave-washed ledges is generally easy in calm weather. A doubled rope is rarely needed to get down.

Cornish granite is so rough-grained that ordinary boots with vibram soles are still the best footwear for general climbing. In Cornwall, Andrews had been the innovator of using plimsolls for rock climbing; thus the use of "rubbers" was given to British mountaineering. The lace-up type of rubber and canvas boot with a comfortably close fit will prove sufficient for more difficult climbing, but for the hardest climbs the universal P.A. type of light boot is needed. The battering of holds from nailed boots of Commandoes in training during the last war is plainly evident on

16. Peter Biven leading Doorpost on the Main Face at Bosigran. The upper part of the route takes fine cracks in an exposed position.

many popular routes. Whereas Cornish granite appears to survive the passage of time and many scraping feet, unlike the worn and bone-smooth holds on scores of routes in mountain areas, future generations will appreciate our gentle use of the rock.

Natural belays on the granite tend to vanish above the "Severe" grade, so that pegs are used on Grade V and VI climbs. Artificial chocks, called "nuts" in the vernacular, serve as most running belays. Trevor Peck developed his "Cracker" in Cornwall and this was the first nut to reach production runs in Britain. As a technique on the rockface the use of nuts is still virtually confined to Britain and has only a small following as yet in Europe and the United States.

Cliffs forming the northern coast of West Penwith are the most frequented in the district. The western aspect of the peninsula, near Land's End, is also quite popular; this coastal stretch was thoroughly explored by Commandos and Marines during and after the last war. On the South coast, Chair Ladder – an imposing castellated buttress on the tip of Tol-Pedn-Penwith headland, is outstanding in an otherwise slightly disappointing part of the granite. Further East climbing on greenstone has been developed, as it has been to some extent on the North coast as well.

One of Andrews' original forays (1902) on the North coast was the ascent of Wicca Pillar. This 60 ft. rock thumb is now of secondary importance because the immediate vicinity does not offer continuous or long climbs. Working to the West along this tortured coast a few routes can be made at Zennor and at Gurnard's Head on greenstone. There are excellent practice climbs and wonderful bathing in Halldrine Cove. In this direction we soon reach the area known collectively as Bosigran where the finest, most varied and longest routes in Cornwall are found.

The main face of Bosigran flanks Porthmoina Cove which is completely hemmed in by steep granite cliffs. The rock scenery is unrivalled in Cornwall. At one end the main face rises inland so that it is generally described in three parts, as the Seaward and Landward Cliffs divided by the Main Cliff. The Landward part was ignored for a long time; it has mainly fine routes of Grade III (Very Difficult), reaching a height of 150 ft., and including one of the best Grade II climbs in Cornwall, Alison Rib. The Main Cliff, over 200 ft. high and standing 300 ft. above the sea, has been the scene of the most important advances in climbing standards in Cornwall, immediately prior to the recent assault on the Great Zawn. High up on its smooth wall the face is cut by a line of

17.   Mark Springett hand-traversing on String of Pearls which girdles the Main Face at Bosigran. He is moving towards the belayed climber, as the normal direction for the route is from right to left when facing the cliff.

irregular overhangs which were rigorously avoided until twenty years ago. The best of the easier routes include Ledge Climb (II+) and Doorway (IV+), while among the harder ones Little Brown Jug (VI—), Thin Wall Special (VI) and Doorpost (V) can be recommended. The main challenge of the face and its attendant overhangs are tackled by Bow Wall (VI/VI+), a line started by Joe Brown who could not finish because his second failed him; Suicide Wall (VI), the most popular route of its class at Bosigran, by the Biven brothers and Trevor Peck, who have contributed so much as a team of two or three to modern Cornish climbing; and Beowulf (VI) and Paragon (VI) by Peter Biven and Peck. Another sensational piece of rock work is the girdle traverse called String of Pearls (VI). It wanders boldly across the centre of the face below the main overhangs for 750 ft. and represents a landmark in the climbing career of John Deacon of the Marine Commando, whose special place in Cornish exploration is seen on Chair Ladder. The traverse was made with Rawdon Goodier. Interesting peg routes include Ghost and Phantom. The Raven Wall original route is now impossible owing to the one crack being full of rusted and broken off pegs. The 150 ft. Seaward Cliff of Bosigran is noted for its fine open climbing at a reasonable standard; the favoured routes are on Ochre Slab (three lines), Black Slab (II—), and Ding (V).

Porthmoina Cove itself is partly occupied by the celebrated Island, called Bosigran Pinnacle by Andrews. It is a huge mass of tapering rock, long and thin, with a sharp crest resembling a pinnacled Alpine ridge. From the mainland a sea-washed boulder bridge is crossed at low water to reach the Island. Most of the climbing, including the ordinary traverse (350 ft., II), is in the lower grades of difficulty. After the traverse, a good expedition is to return across the West Face. There is also an amusing girdle of the Island.

The South side of the Cove is enclosed by the equally famous Bosigran or Commando Ridge. Starting from sea-level, and after dodging a few waves, the ridge gives 700 ft. of Grade III climbing with soft options to suit the ability of most parties, and hard ones for purists. Beyond the secondary parallel Western Ridge the coastal cliff is cut by a deep narrow inlet called the Great Zawn. A steep scramble leads down the West side of the entrance, but the opposite side is difficult of access. The pioneers were unable to find a convenient way across the mouth of the zawn at any level. On the East side an entrance using rope tactics was

18.   A new route called Liberator on the wall of the Great Zawn, made by Frank Cannings and Pat Littlejohn in 1970. The climb is considered the hardest at Bosigran.

64

19. *Chair Ladder from the west, at low water. The obvious line of Western Chimneys can be seen immediately right of the Great Gully, and the Red Wall route goes up in steps to the right again.*

achieved by Andrews in 1923, along the Green Cormorant Ledge. But only in 1956 was this entrance effected "cleanly" by the Biven brothers and Peck. Above the ledge the wall of the zawn can be climbed by the Green Cormorant Face (VI, A2), a route by John Deacon and Mike Banks, though climbed free in 1969. After this more routes on its walls were made by artificial means, and after 1968 a new series was begun resulting in several free climbs of VI+. These are the most difficult climbs in Cornwall, pioneered by Cannings, Littlejohn and Martin Jones.

The remaining cliffs of Bosigran are somewhat broken. There are short climbs of some merit on Rosemergy Ridge and round Brandy's Zawn. Portheras Cove is a favourite spot for family gatherings and appropriate short climbs. Nothing further of great interest appears until we round the corner of Cape Cornwall and reach the West coast at Land's End. The entire area is known to climbers as the Sennen Cliffs and is strategically well-placed for retiring to the pubs and cafés of Sennen. The first headland above Land's End is Pedn-Mên-Du; it has a varied collection of routes of up to 100 ft. in all standards of difficulty. On the Land's End headland some of the rock is suspect in quality, but the locality includes one of the best Grade III climbs in the country: Johnstone's Route. On the whole the climbs fall short of 100 ft. The main ridge route is Long Climb (220 ft., III). These headlands in the vicinity of Land's End in summer are swarming with tourists with their feet or bottoms planted firmly on the ground. Climbing with an audience may not be a unique experience in outcrop work, but the hazard at Land's End is litter and ducking to avoid carelessly tossed bottles. The next interesting headland is Pordenack, with fewer but a similar variety of climbs. This is succeeded by Carn Boel and Carn Lês Boel, where the coast starts to turn eastwards. The pinnacled crest of the Carn Lês Boel promontory was first traversed in 1912 by Winthrop Young and G. L. Mallory of the later Everest drama. As well as harbouring large nesting areas of gulls these cliffs contain near-inaccessible caves frequented by seals during breeding. The photograph of the Bosistow Island Stack at Carn Lês Boel is taken from the main cave zawn which can only be entered by swimming. An underwater camera was taken on this expedition.

Just before the cliffs round Hella Point and turn completely South-facing, we reach the Tol-Pedn-Penwith headland and Chair Ladder. Rising directly from the sea for over 200 ft. this is easily the most picturesque rock pile in Cornwall. It consists of about eight separate castellated buttresses divided down the middle by the main descent line of Ash Can Gully. The Chair Ladder of most photographs, including ours, is the western half, shown as a pillar detached from the main cliff by Great Gully which falls into a zawn. Major areas of rock continue on

either side of the buttresses, so that altogether the cliff forms an imposing bastion.

An important feature of Chair Ladder climbing is the ledges crossing most of the buttresses at various levels. While these provide convenient access points on to the sea face they can also be used as escape exits from some of the best routes, thereby tending to reduce the seriousness of the cliff. This situation is further aggravated by the closeness of comparatively easy and much harder routes which rise a few feet apart to the summit. Yet the abiding steepness and the characteristic perfect rock compensate for these deficiencies.

The Western Chimneys were climbed before the First World War by Andrews and Prof. J. E. Littlewood independently of each other. The professor's later investigations went unrecorded for over forty years, while his parties seem to have been the only visits up to 1935. By this time the more obvious lines had been discovered and climbed; notably Central Buttress Chimneys (III) and the top section of Pendulum Chimney. During and immediately after the Second World War Marine Commandoes made a series of fine routes, Flannel Avenue (V) being outstanding. But the route of the period and now the classic ascent at Chair Ladder was South Face Direct (V+) in 1948 by J. Cortlandt-Simpson and E. Stones. There are now visible signs of wear and tear on the climb, and its standard has been raised accordingly. More climbs of this calibre soon materialised. From 1954 the name of John Deacon remains prominent, culminating after five years in the magnificently exposed Excelsior (VI).

Chair Ladder is refreshingly free from climbing with artificial aids, except for belays and protection. The locality does not have as much variety as Bosigran, but there are several worthwhile routes on the nearby Hella Point. It is claimed that the Ladder has fallen out of favour. The few leaders of Cornish climbing are certainly looking elsewhere for new routes, but the ordinary traffic to the cliff is undiminished.

20. *Bosistow Island, a stack in the cove under Carn Lês Boel. The climber is reaching it from the mainland cliffs by a Tyrolean traverse. The sea cave from which the photograph was taken can only be reached by swimming; there are new routes on its right wall, looking out.*

5 Lundy

Access: From Ilfracombe (24 miles) and Swansea (32 miles to Ilfracombe) or Cardiff, and from other North Devon resorts connecting to the first, by steam vessel three or four times a week in summer; journey of $1\frac{3}{4}$ hours from Ilfracombe; open tender used to reach landing beach.
Accommodation: Manor Farm Hotel, by prior arrangement only and with consent of the Resident Agent, Lundy, Bristol Channel.
Camping: Applications in writing to the Resident Agent. Water is available.
Facilities: Shop and public house. Parties which have arranged to stay on the island are advised to arrive as far as possible self-sufficient.
Earliest recorded climbs: 1892.
Maps: O.S. One Inch, Sheet 163. O.S. $2\frac{1}{2}$ Inch, Sheet SS 44. Six Inch special map. David & Charles, 1970.
Climbing guidebook: Moulton, R. D., *Lundy Rock Climbs*, Royal Navy M.C., 1970.

The Norsemen called it *Lund-Eye*, Isle of Puffins – a low blue shape floating off Devon on the line where the sea meets the sky. Other Scandinavian names interpret it as "Grove Island". Stronghold of robber-barons, lair of Turkish pirates, cavaliers retreat, smugglers' refuge, penal settlement and tomb of countless ships, history has swirled round Lundy as do the tide races of the wild Atlantic. Today Lundy is a peaceful anacronism, not quite a private kingdom and not quite part of Devon. It issues its own postage stamps and its tavern obeys no Licensing Justices. On its one lane the only traffic is a farm tractor and all access to the island is dependent on the moods of the sea. As islands go its quality is rare, but to the climber Lundy is unique.

Sitting astride the entrance to the Bristol Channel, 12 miles North of Hartland Point and some 30 miles South-West of Gower, Lundy is like a compass needle just three miles long and half a mile in width. It is an exposed and rolling plateau covered with bracken, heather and rough pasture and rising to an extreme elevation of 470 ft. The eastern flanks, slopes of deep bracken and rhododendron, fall steeply into clear green water. But to the West the ground ends in a complex line of great crags which drop sheer into a restless sea. The far South-East corner of the island, where the landing beach is situated, and where the church, the tavern and farm buildings huddle, is composed of grey slates similar to the

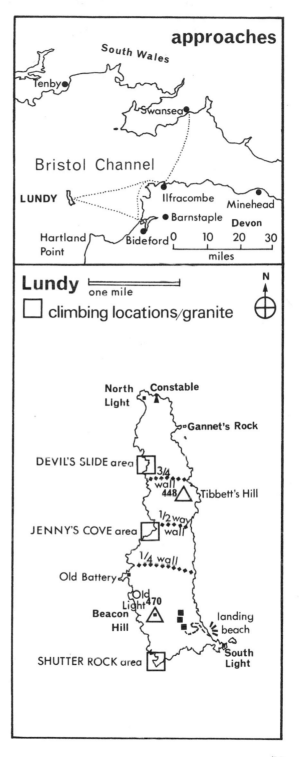

approaches

South Wales

Tenby●

Swansea●

Bristol Channel

LUNDY

Ilfracombe●

Minehead●

●Barnstaple

Devon

Hartland
Point

Bideford●

0   10   20   30

miles

Lundy   ⊢━━━━┤
            one mile

N

☐ climbing locations/granite

North   Constable
Light

●Gannet's Rock

DEVIL'S SLIDE area

¾
wall

448

Tibbett's Hill

½ way
wall

JENNY'S COVE area

¼ wall

Old Battery

Old
Light 470

Beacon
Hill

landing
beach

South
Light

SHUTTER ROCK area

loose shales of the North Devon coast. The rest of the island however is a solid chunk of red granite, giving superb climbing akin to that of the Bosigran Face in Cornwall but with much more variation – and of course there is much more of it. Most crags rise straight from the sea and there can be access problems due to the high Bristol Channel tides.

The island plateau is crossed by three walls, dividing it roughly into four, which make useful landmarks. The cultivation is to the South of Quarter Wall, where there are fields of hay and cattle grazing, and in the sheltered Millcombe the only trees on Lundy. Besides the buildings already mentioned there is the Trinity House South Light, Marisco Castle – the ancestral home of the buccaneer ruler-owners in days gone by, Millcombe House, a few cottages, and on the island's summit, Beacon Hill, the disused 97 ft. tower of the Old Light. The rough track known to climbers as the "L.1", and marked all its length with large stone blocks as a guide in mist, leads northward through Quarter Wall, past the ruins of old quarrymen's cottages, through Halfway Wall and over the brow of Tibbett's Hill with its old look-out to Threequarter Wall. Beyond is the North End, the roughest moorland on Lundy, where there are ruins of a Bronze Age settlement and – at the far tip – the North Light.

Until recently Lundy was the personal property of Mr Albion Harman. On his death it was purchased by the conservationist millionaire, Jack Hayward, for the National Trust, and is now being managed for them by the Landmark Trust. Thus the island is a private estate and access is carefully controlled. During the summer months White Funnel steamers make several trips each week from Ilfracombe, Cardiff and other Bristol Channel ports, carrying principally day-trip tourists. As the steamers have a bar and restaurant aboard they make the journey easier for the serious visitor than does the usual island tender, the MFV Lundy Gannet, which runs out of Ilfracombe each week throughout the year, weather permitting. There is no harbour on Lundy, so passengers and their baggage are taken off the steamer in small open boats. The trip from Ilfracombe takes about 1¾ hours and the fare one way in 1971 was £1.60. Although few trippers get further than the Village Green with its tavern and shop, it is possible for a swift party to climb the famous Devil's Slide in the three hours allowed ashore.

21.   Flying Buttress, an easy classic on Lundy located below the Battery on the west coast, not far from the Old Light. The rocky skerry from which it rises is only accessible at half-tide. On the opposite, South, face is Diamond Solitaire, and on the walls to north and south are several other 150 ft. routes.

Anyone wishing to stay on the island should write beforehand to the Resident Agent to ask for permission and to inquire about accommodation and sailings. Climbers, though welcomed, should note that certain cliffs are out-of-bounds during the nesting season from mid-May to the end of July. A charge of 25 pence per night is levied for camping, which is excellent, but many climbers will prefer the hut-type self-cooking facilities of the Old Light building. Otherwise there is country-style Manor Farm Hotel and a few holiday cottages which can be rented. The hub of island life is the tavern, and close-by is the shop which sells most food and camping stores. Climbing apart, Lundy is ideal for a short, quiet, away-from-it-all family holiday. And for climbers it is just the perfect place to forget the crowded pubs and rope-knitted rockfaces of our mountains in Wales and Cumberland.

Most sea cliff climbing is serious from the rescue point of view, and Lundy is no exception. A Thomas stretcher has been supplied, with 600 ft. of rope in late 1971. There is also radio communication with the mainland, and a R.A.F. helicopter, dependent on the weather for its long over-sea journey, is the only swift means of casualty evacuation. An accident in August 1971 proved that a team of experienced climbers can get a serious casualty from the bottom of an awkward zawn into a helicopter in three hours, but only aided by every man on the island and in ideal conditions. On this occasion the aircraft was later forced to ditch at sea with engine trouble and it was only by extraordinary luck that the injured man was not drowned.

The climbing history of Lundy is as old as that of any other British sea cliff area. The first known ascent was that of the Constable, an impressive spire near the North Light, in 1881 by an unknown – and possibly drunken – sailor. Today his route is graded IV. There are two other harder and longer lines on this granite column and further potential on its North face. Perhaps the Gannet's Rock, a massive 150 ft. stack off the North-East corner of Lundy, was climbed in the Middle Ages, for its gannet harvest then was valued at five shillings. The route to the summit, though thin and exposed for a few feet, is only Grade II+. However, it was certainly climbed by the ubiquitous Tom Longstaff in the 1890s on his first visit to Lundy when he also climbed on St James' Stone. He was the first serious climber to appear on the scene and he returned in 1903 and again in 1927.

22.   Keith Darbyshire on the final pitch and crux of Albion. This pitch is one of the finest on the island – thin slab climbing and laybacks in the corner-crack, protected with the occasional good nut.

It is surprising that no other climbers realised Lundy's potential once the Cornish granite had been discovered. It was not until 1960 that Admiral Lawder and Ted Pyatt made the next climbing reconnaissance during a day-trip. They were back the following year with a small but strong party and climbed the now classic Devil's Slide, a fabulous 400 ft. slab at about Grade IV+. Gannet's Buttress, a very bold 230 ft. route of Grade VI situated opposite the stack, with the crux on the last few moves in an aerial position on a holdless overhang, and still one of the hardest routes on Lundy, fell to the party, as did the two major sea stacks. The Devil's Chimney (130 ft., V+) is a fine tidal pinnacle below beetling 300 ft. walls, and the smaller and easier 70 ft. Needle Rock, a very maritime stack, are also well worth climbing.

By 1962 Peter Biven, one of the leading contenders in British sea cliff climbing, had discovered Lundy. With Cliff Fishwick he found another easy classic, Flying Buttress, a huge natural arch immediately below the Old Battery, which still has its rusty 18-pounder cannon. Their return the next year resulted in a crop of routes, most notably Albion (400 ft., VI), named for the then owner, which Biven climbed leading through with Viv Stevenson. This fine route takes the groove between the left edge of the Devil's Slide and the wall overhanging it. The same year Tony Smythe and John Cleare repeated routes and made further explorations, while Hughie Banner was active about the same time. Unfortunately the Old Light log book has been lost and with it the record of those early days.

The next six years produced a steady trickle of new climbs. In 1967 a Lundy Supplement to the Royal Navy M.C.'s Devonshire guide appeared. Notable routes from this period are Diamond Solitaire (VI), a delicate and bottomless slab on the South face of Flying Buttress, climbed by an Army Outward Bound School party; and Stingray (VI+), for some time the hardest climb on the island – a contribution from the Bradford University Club.

For 1970 Bob Moulton wrote a new guide for the Navy Club, this time to Lundy alone. But that year saw Biven back at work, in company with Ian Howell. They opened up the magnificent vertical wall of Shutter Buttress, directly opposite the Great Shutter Rock immortalised by Charles Kingsley in *Westward Ho!*, and near the resting place of the

23. *The 400 ft. slab of the Devil's Slide must be unique south of Scotland. Today there are several lines on it, none of them easier than Grade IV. Peter Biven is seen on one of the harder variations. Beyond are the twin peaks of St James's Stone – almost islands – on which there is good scrambling.*

dreadnought HMS *Montague*. Then they forced the nearby Devil's Lime Kiln. This was a tour-de-force, and is undoubtedly one of the greatest sea cliff routes in the country. Although only technically Grade V its 400 ft. "depth" is inescapable and the climb is a serious one. The Kiln is a huge blow-hole – which legend says was left when the Devil scooped out the Great Shutter Rock itself from the clifftop. Its bottom is reached through a long and narrow cave at low tide below the Shutter Buttress.

In the meantime other West Country aces were busy. In a brief weekend Frank Cannings and Pat Littlejohn produced several hard routes on the West coast, perhaps the best of which are Littlejohn's Albacore (VI+) on the buttress below the Old Light, and Canning's Magnificat (VI+) on the great Devil's Buttress – surely the dominating crag on the North-West of the island.

More was to come in 1971. Keith Darbyshire and Biven powered the West Arête of the Constable by a fierce technical line they called The Summons (VI+), and went on to force the Shark, the hardest route yet made on Lundy, on the left-bounding arête of the Slide and overhanging Albion; it is a desperate line with a series of exacting lay-back moves for the crux. Odd Eliassen, the Norwegian climber, and John Cleare climbed Bloodaxe (VI) on the Castle – the long buttress opposite St John's Stone, while Ken Wilson discovered The Seventh Seal (VI−) on the great wall to the North of Shark, a route destined surely to become a classic of the future. Already the 1970 Guide was out of date and Lundy climbing had come of age. It will undoubtedly follow the patterns traced in Cornwall and much remains to be done.

24. *Devil's Chimney, a fine 130 ft. stack of flawless granite, rises from the sea on the southern rim of Jenny's Cove. It can be approached below half-tide and the route leads via overhanging cracks just above the climbers to the final wall.*

Overleaf:

25. *Devil's Lime Kiln. On the thin top pitch of this unique climb of 400 ft. out of the bowels of the earth. You start in darkness in a black chimney and work upward in four long pitches into the sun.*

26. *Off the far southern point of Jenny's Cove stands Needle Rock. Accessible dryfoot at low tides, the easiest route (III) goes round the corner to the right. There are several harder routes to the tiny summit.*

6 North Devon

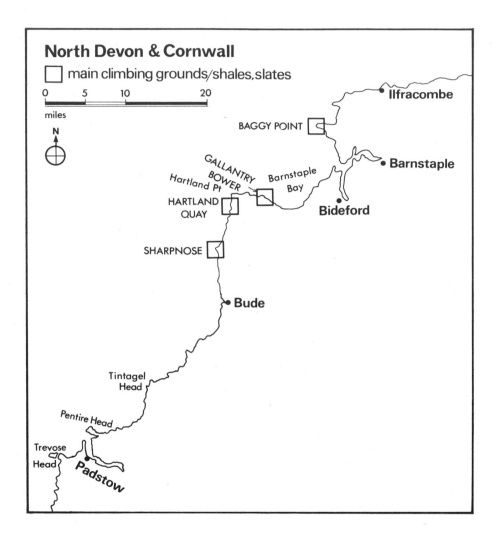

North Devon & Cornwall

☐ main climbing grounds/shales, slates

0   5   10   20

miles

N

Ilfracombe

BAGGY POINT

Barnstaple

GALLANTRY BOWER

Hartland Pt

Barnstaple Bay

HARTLAND QUAY

Bideford

SHARPNOSE

Bude

Tintagel Head

Pentire Head

Trevose Head

Padstow

Climbing potential in North Devon is roughly divided by the huge re-entrant of Barnstaple Bay. The bay apart, this causes the coastline to fall into two parts. To the North and East are many miles of hogs-back cliff scenery, like a small mountain range in configuration with individual summits, marking the northern edge of Exmoor Forest. To the South and West the cliffs are mainly flat-topped, and continue southwards into Cornwall. Coastal waterfalls, the outlets for numerous short rivers, spring straight into the sea from cliffs in both parts. Similar sights can be seen only in Scotland.

The northern coastline, running from the Foreland near Lynton to Baggy Point inside the bay, has emerged in recent times as the Eiger of an activity aptly described as "coasteering". A coasteer is one who practises this pastime. There are so few people who could justify the title that the originators and their disciples comprise almost the entire company, past and present.

The cliffs of the North coast are of Old Red Sandstone, a poor rock hereabouts, and variable slates, and the hogs-back elevation screens them from above. There is no clifftop path in the ordinary sense, and dense brambly vegetation and ferns covering the seaward side of this "roof" prevent easy access to the cliffs below. It was just because of this natural concealment of the lower seaward cliffs and their unvisited beaches, or whatever, that a few men were inspired to unravel the mysteries of this rugged coast.

As a boy, the explorer Tom Longstaff had traversed parts of the North coast at sea-level before 1900, as Andrews had in Cornwall. In his autobiography he relates: "The cliffs are only slate but finely fretted by tumultuous seas. We began climbing in a small way in 1887 and by 1892 we were using a rope. Such climbs were nearly all horizontal traverses. The rules were to get round the headlands between the top of the cliffs and the sea below, keeping above high water mark if possible." Following this reference, which did not reach the light of day until 1950, the cliffs were not looked at again closely until 1954. The late C. H. Archer and a companion then began an exploration in traversing that lasted ten years. Climbers did not become aware of this great adventure until it was almost complete. Only then did Archer learn of his antecedents, in Longstaff and Andrews. The conscientious field-worker and historian, E. C. Pyatt, established that coasteering in the grand style, as exampled by the traverse of the fore- and back-shores of North Devon, involves maritime knowledge and matters of judgement quite distinct from mountaineering standards. Technical difficulty on steep rock was generally avoided. Yet such were the complications that faced Archer and his later companions that a new scale of problems peculiar to coasteering arose. The cliff structures and beach terrain are enormously varied. In the absence of frequent descent routes, escape upwards was rarely easy during the exploratory years. The party learnt, a few hundred yards at a time, of the area of cliff and shore that was swept between normal and abnormal tides. The ground to be crossed and headlands to be won

27.   *The cliffs at Baggy Point, looking from the southern side to the highest point, about 350 ft. above the boulder beach.*

changed frequently and were frequently changed by the rising and falling sea. Every yard of this intricate coastline was fought for in route planning and route finding, till all the pieces fitted like a jigsaw.

A few enthusiasts believe that coasteering will become popular and has a big future. It is the most logical approach to cliff-foot traverses in the chalk areas described in Chapter One. The locations of the great sea cliff traverses on limestone can be mainly ruled out because shorelines are seldom exposed for any distance, although a route like the Lulworth Traverse can be counted as falling midway between the two ideas. Significantly, only a few conventional climbs have been made to date on the North Devon coast. We have to enter Barnstaple Bay and come to Baggy Point before signs of modern sea cliff climbing appear.

Baggy Point, standing about 300 ft. above the sea, was the scene of the first rock climb put up in North Devon. Longstaff turned one of the secondary projections of the headland by climbing a conspicuous corner/crack, which he called Scrattling Crack (150 ft., II+). The rock is brittle sandstone and the complex zawn-indented foot of the headland is riddled with caves. A series of some twenty routes of high calibre were suddenly made in 1969 and 1970 by climbers from London. Reports at the time suggested that Biven and Littlejohn, who had been there first, had missed the real challenges of the headland, and were criticised for taking a flippant attitude in looking for new rock in the county. While routes of 300 ft. were forced up the loose slabs and walls at Baggy Point, the inconsistency of the rock was upheld after return visits. One exception, according to Littlejohn, is Pink Void (VI), which he compared in character and quality with Moonraker in South Devon.

When we come to examine the lower or western and southern part of the coast – soon crossing into the county of Cornwall, many more attempts to unearth sea cliff climbing have been recorded. Down to Tintagel Head, cliffs are frequent. They are composed mainly of carboniferous grits and shales in which the strata is greatly distorted because of the rapid marine erosion taking place. Further West again many other rock types occur along the coast – most of them completely unsuitable for climbing. E. M. Hazelton scrambled on the photogenic folded rock faces near Bude during the Second World War and reported: "The cliffs are friable, treacherous and end at their summits in yards of bare soil." Despite the fact that there are now some fifty routes spaced out at intervals along this part of the coast, interest at present is fairly static. Only the most insatiable appetite for virgin rock sallies forth on new ventures. Pat Littlejohn can always be relied on for making signs of a revival. He has recently "rediscovered" Gallantry Bower on the South side of Barnstaple Bay, about two miles from Clovelly. The true landmark

85

is a horrible grass slope 350 ft. high and 60° steep. But further West is a 250 ft. shale cliff consisting of high-angle slabs offset by overlapping corners, looking like the famous West Buttress of Cloggy in Snowdonia. A VI+ route has been put up here by Littlejohn, and there are two or three easier lines. Nearby, the foreshore stack called Black Church Rock has been done by a hard slab route.

The main section of this coast runs South from Hartland Point, where the Bristol Channel becomes the real Atlantic Ocean. Ted Pyatt recorded two or three routes on this stretch in 1957 and the first dare-devil climbs were made in 1959 by the great Scottish mountaineer, Tom Patey. His Wrecker's Slab (350 ft., VI) on Cornakey Cliff has seldom been repeated and has defeated several parties due to the unnerving nature of the rock. Pinnacles standing on the foreshore have attracted a lot of attention. The best known is perhaps Bear Rock at Hartland Quay. It has been climbed by two routes, the first in 1962 being called Barely Possible (80 ft., III+). South of this point, and beyond the waterfall of Speke's Mill Mouth, are Cornakey Cliff, Vicarage Cliff and the Higher and Lower Sharpnose headlands. Some of their faces rise close to 400 ft. above the sea but the outcome of an attempt to reach the top is always uncertain. Once when Littlejohn was convinced that he had found a sure line, and had started up on what appeared to be a pitch of good rock, at 15 ft. above the start the slabby mass on which he was poised suddenly collapsed without warning and he found himself at the bottom again among a heap of rock rubble. The entire face below him had broken away like a small snow avalanche. It follows that most of the successful climbs made to date are in the easier grades. Ted Pyatt contends that the western coasts of North Devon and Cornwall are a major climbing area. From the evidence of exploration carried out so far we feel bound to disagree, and are supported in this view by resident authorities of unrivalled experience such as John Fowler and Peter Biven. Certainly there are cliffs that the present generation have dismissed as preposterous or impossible. The wall of sandstone about 600 ft. high under the Great Hangman on the North coast has been so described. It is not just a matter of loose rock and unpleasant rock formations. The quality and character of routes that might be made seems in doubt. This coastline is too varied geologically to produce in the future more than isolated climbing of merit. As far down in Cornwall as Padstow and Newquay, Messrs. Cleare, Fowler and Littlejohn have scoured the shoreline for promising sea pinnacles and stacks. Attempts on the Merope

28.   Offshore stacks at Bedruthan Steps, North Cornwall.

Rocks on Trevose Head and beach rocks in the bay of Bedruthan Steps have been successful recently despite loosely jointed slate and shales.

It would be safer to predict that coasteering has a more promising future in the neighbourhood. So far as we are aware no one has attempted to classify the problems of traversing the sea shore from Hartland Point down to say Trevose Head. Though Archer and his friends were exceptions in achieving the passage of the northern coastline, further development in this field is only likely to come from people with climbing experience. The danger is that one day coasteering might become common knowledge and lure some of the many thousands of holidaymakers on the beaches into attempting "walks" beyond the frequented bathing reaches.

29. (previous page) Biven's Route, adjoining Scrattling Crack on Baggy Point in North Devon.

30. An unclimbed stack at Gunver Head, being approached by a Tyrolean rope manoeuvre.

7   Gower Peninsula

Access: Railway to Swansea. Frequent bus services by United Welsh to all parts of the peninsula in 20 miles or less. Bus No. 13 from Swansea serves most of the approaches to the main cliffs.

Accommodation: Inns and hotels in all villages, and a fair number of houses and cottages to rent.

Camping: Large camping sites and caravan parks have sprung up all over Gower in the last 10 years, but the authorities have now restricted this growth (a number of fines were imposed in 1969). The main public sites are at Port-eynon and Rhossili, while many smaller ones are annexed to farms and private property. Camping on the downland at the clifftops is tempting (wonderful locations in sheltered dells free from vegetation and undergrowth) but strictly forbidden everywhere.

Facilities: General stores in all village centres.

Earliest recorded climbs: 1949 (now disputed).

Maps: O.S. One Inch, Sheets 152, 153. O.S. $2\frac{1}{2}$ Inch, Sheets SS 48, 49, 58. One Inch Visitor's Map. Geographia Ltd.

Guidebook: Talbot, J. O., *Gower Peninsula*, West Col Productions, 1970.

In the British mountaineering scene, be it on the mountains or the sea cliffs, Gower is the lost child of a multiplying family. It was recently estimated that a mere 200 climbers live in the industrial belt of South Wales between Newport and Swansea. Yet this is more than the number estimated for Devon and Cornwall, where thousands come to the granite of West Penwith in summer. While Gower for the average climber is expressly the most suitable – and scenically the finest – of the limestone coastal regions of Britain, it was never "found" and publicised in the manner we know for other newly developed areas. The Gower enigma is the antithesis say of Dorset limestone, with its rude bare coastline and short but concentrated history of climbing eulogy. Perhaps it is no coincidence that a similar situation has obtained in general tourism until recent times. Gower had been the jealously-guarded Shangri-La of a few well informed holidaymakers (it is said from Lancashire). Robin Collomb was introduced to a Swansea resident who had never been to Rhossili at the tip of the Gower Peninsula, while an elderly lady who runs a camping site near glorious Oxwich Bay told him that

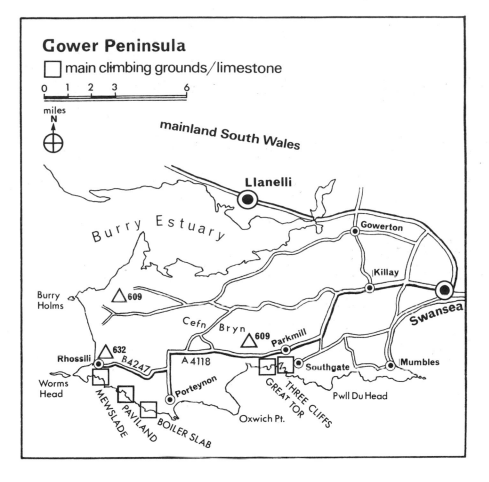

Gower Peninsula

☐ main climbing grounds/limestone

0 1 2 3   6
miles
N

mainland South Wales

Llanelli

Burry Estuary

Gowerton

Killay

Burry Holms

△609

Cefn Bryn

△609 Parkmill

Swansea

Rhossili

△632
B4247

A4118

Southgate

Mumbles

Worms Head

MEWSLADE

PAVILAND

Porteynon

BOILER SLAB

THREE CLIFFS

GREAT TOR

Oxwich Pt.

Pwll Du Head

she had never been to Swansea, only twenty miles away. The common explanation for this extraordinary situation is that no one came on the scene who could grasp the scope for climbing and broadcast it further afield. This much we now know for certain is a wrong assumption.

Though not the first to climb in Gower, a young Swansea man called Jeremy Talbot had been using the sea cliffs since 1958 as a keep-fit gymnasium and practice ground for his major interest in Alpine mountaineering. His pioneering took place in a vacuum, for in Gower he was insulated from the hurly-burly of climbing world gossip and competition. More communicative climbers had preceded him, among them John Brailsford and H. Insley, but the articles and route information they published in the fifties did not inspire any general movement towards the district. With a few exceptions Talbot became the solo explorer, recorder and archivist of Gower climbing – being nearly all his own routes running into hundreds – while the rest of the country remained oblivious of these activities. Throughout this period it must be remembered that his primary interest lay in improving his own standard and techniques for making expeditions in the Alps. Only later was he attracted by the idea of classifying the routes for themselves. The Alpine influence in nomenclature is stronger here because of Talbot than anywhere else in the country. Names derived from calcareous rock-types and features of the Dolomites and the Northern Limestone Ranges of Bavaria and Austria give an unusual colour and atmosphere to the climbing. Hoarding this wealth of experience and knowledge has caused resentment among other resident climbers. It transpires that Jeremy Talbot is not motivated by modern conventions which are inclined to thrive on the chase to find new rock and competitive behaviour. Neither is he secretive by nature nor reticent in good company. Like many other all-round mountaineers in the strict sense of the term, his view reaches beyond the compass of the rock climbing specialist. Mountaineering adventures are essentially a private concern, and you are free to share them with whom you please. He dislikes the trend towards regimentation and personal publicity for captains of the modern movement. Among all the top climbers interviewed and photographed for this book, Jeremy Talbot was the quickest up climbs, and John Cleare was hard pressed to get his camera in position to catch him in action. Cleare felt that he had a duty to chase him, and some amusing incidents occurred when Talbot was asked to stand still on the crux of climbs. He was also vigorously pursued to publish his guidebook. After two years of persuasion the volume materialised in 1970.

In an interview on Gower climbing Talbot unwittingly revealed perhaps the most astonishing mode of development of any rock climbing ground in Britain. The pattern in British rock climbing had always been more or less the same up and down the country. Practice began on outcrops and led to a high standard of technical proficiency. Being close to the ground there was not much to be afraid of. In turn the climber took his knowledge and experience to the mountains and endeavoured to repeat his outcrop performances. The vast majority of people could not reach the same standard. The length of climbs, additional exposure, bad weather and the grander and more remote setting in mountains combined to work against the levels of achievement attained on short rockfaces. A climber's standard of ability was therefore lower in the mountains. If he took the next step and visited the Alps, the scale of undertakings in a glaciated range was such that his technical standard (and much else besides) was likely to fall even further. Yet in Gower exactly the reverse procedure operated. Talbot and his few companions were completely

94

31. The enchanting pile of Three Cliffs, seen across its bay at low water from the foot of Great Tor.

inhibited by steep limestone rock. They rarely visited mountain areas, which might have provided comparisons or a yardstick. At this time one of Talbot's friends who had climbed in North Wales on several occasions had a decisive influence on the group's outlook; unless one was convinced that a climber possessed superior ability routes that looked harder than "V. Diff" (about Grade III) should not be attempted. Consequently this "rule" dominated Gower activity and only a few climbs above this standard were made. It was also the ruling attitude in North Wales and elsewhere until the big break-through was achieved in 1959. It was only after Talbot began a series of holidays in Switzerland that the outlook in Gower changed. He climbed mainly on limestone in the Oberland and Grimsel districts with Swiss guides of the calibre of Hilti von Allmen and Martin Epp. The result was that Talbot returned home with grade V and VI Alpine routes under his belt. He declared to the incredulous small band of peninsula devotees that they had not even started to realise the potential of rockfaces in their own backyard. In no time at all Gower climbing went up in standard by two or three grades. Practising artificial techniques, previously shunned as wicked and unethical, flourished and the rock was soon littered with abandoned pegs and slings. Later arrivals in Gower from more distant parts of the country mistook the rusting and rotting ironmongery planted in rock as the handiwork of inexperienced local climbers. Talbot removed most of the evidence from "bolt" routes – probably for financial reasons! – and left the newcomers and others to squabble among themselves as to which routes justified the use of pegs. On all the occasions we have accompanied him in the district, doing climbs up to the hardest grades, he has never placed a peg – though that is not to say that we did not use a peg already found in place. We missed the weekend when, it is said, a visitor was caught tapping out a protection peg from a particularly difficult traverse. The climber was having to retreat from the position but thought he would collect something for his trouble. He was being watched, and after Talbot had blistered him with words he left empty-handed. The situation today is that all the main climbing grounds are "patrolled" by Jeremy Talbot. He is there nearly every weekend and nearly every evening as well in summer, furthering exploration, tidying up the rockfaces, throwing down ropes to spreadeagled climbers, offering advice, leading parties caught

32. Jeremy Talbot on the top section of Gefion on King Wall. This is possibly the most popular cliff in Gower, rising from fine sands to the Great Terrace below Lewes Castle. The line of Fall Bay is seen behind.

97

by the tide off the beaches to safety. He is clearly not pleased with the newly found popularity of Gower.

There is no record of climbing in Gower before the 1939–45 war. At first it was thought that the Osborn brothers' ascent of Boiler Slab in 1949 marked the start. It now seems that military personnel may have made routes during the war, including the famous East Ridge of Great Tor, which to date is credited to the Osborns during 1952. Whatever findings are published by Talbot in the future, the fact remains that Gower belongs to the post-war boom, and in this respect much of the climbing is more in keeping with the leisurely – even casual – proceedings of the 1920s and 30s.

Historically the peninsula has belonged to titled English families and became part of Glamorgan in 1535. The characteristically agricultural English part of Gower lies to the South and South-West of its central downland ridge of Cefn Bryn. The boundary nearly coincides with the outcrop of the Coal Measures, with the industrial and Welsh-speaking population on the North side. Therefore stretching west of Swansea the peninsula is composed of folded Old Red Sandstone along its hilly backbone while most of the southern part is of Mountain or Carboniferous Limestone covered inland by boulder clay. The limestone sea cliffs are of great beauty and reveal perfectly exposed examples of vertical folding. Caves along the coast are noted for their pre-historic animal remains and man-worked flints. A partial skeleton was discovered in the famous one at Paviland which, after false identification as a woman, was of a man judged to have lived about 20,000 years ago. The striking cliff scenery of the entire South coast is enhanced by exceptionally beautiful sandy bays, some large, some small. Hillocks and grassy slopes run down to the very edge of these, and different parts are separated by prominent headlands and castle-like tors.

In Gower there is often a second rockface above the beach level cliff. Springing from steep hillsides these upper cliffs are sometimes quite loose and they have been largely ignored by climbers. Some of them have produced surprisingly good routes now that the psychological fear of them has been overcome.

The coast along its southern, western and northern outlooks is liberally sprinkled with cliffs of all shapes and sizes. The more interesting southern

33.   A lower sea-washed face, the Devil's Wall, Mewslade, is another frequented practice cliff. Like so many routes on limestone in this area, even easy ones such as White Lime shown here are vertical or overhanging, but the holds are large and comforting. Thurba Head is beyond.

sections have upper and lower cliff paths on National Trust property. These walks conduct you through some of the finest sea cliff scenery in Britain and are a useful educational preliminary for locating the whereabouts of particular crags.

Limestone, as we have emphasised elsewhere, comes in various degrees of solidity and structural form. The geological idea of exposed strata predominates in this region, where the folding can be seen openly, in contrast say to South Devon, where the rock at first sight might be anything. The lower cliffs, rising from sea level, are dark in colour due to marine erosion. The rock texture is uncommonly rough. It also gives remarkably good holds and, unusually for limestone, has excellent frictional properties. The rock is absolutely clean for as much as 100 ft. above the sea, which is an indication of the height to which waves can rise in stormy weather, while seaweed, marine crustations and slimy conditions are virtually unknown. We believe this is due to the predominance of sandy beaches. Above all the vertical is the norm. The upper cliffs present another picture. With white and grey rock the material is easily recognised as Mountain Limestone. It is severely jointed, vegetation flourishes in fissures and crannies, and a lot of it is intrinsically loose. However these cliffs are now affording some of the best modern-style routes; after "gardening" solid rock and good holds appear, but the constant factor of steepness and exposure make them serious undertakings. Jeremy Talbot's excavations on the upper cliffs can be compared in determination with Bentley Beetham's in Borrowdale thirty years ago.

So wide and extensive is the area of climable rock in Gower that we must confine our remarks to the best climbing grounds on the South coast of the peninsula. Working West along the seaboard from Swansea and Mumbles the headlands near Pennard rise step-like from the sea and offer a mixed bag of routes, mainly on the upper tiers. The late Eryl Pardoe was responsible for much of the modern development here. His Sudan (VI) and Phraetic Line (VI+) are classics. The standard route of the district is Alpha (V−), of 1958 vintage by H. Insley. It is not until we reach Pobbles Bay on the East side of Three Cliffs that the tourist throngs are encountered. Access is from Southgate or Pennard across a golf course. Three Cliffs, as the name fails to imply, consists of an isolated rock promontory jutting at an angle into the sea. Three shapely "summits"

34. Climbers and spectators silhouetted against the evening light on Lewes Castle. The South-East Pillar of this great rock is one of the trade routes of Gower. The bulge of rock between the two climbers has fallen down since this photograph was taken, making the ascent more difficult.

are formed along its ridge (hence the name), which give a pleasant scramble, and the climbing face is on the seaward side. At exceptional low water the base dries out to a huge strand (see illustration) on all sides, but it is possible to traverse on to the face at most states of the tide. The most conspicuous feature is the natural cave arch under the col between the landward and central summits. From the outside, Scavenger (100 ft., V−), the classic route of the face, goes up on to a smooth delicate slab with small holds forming the top of the arch. On the whole the numerous climbs are in the easier grades and up to 150 ft. in length.

A river outfall, which can be waded when the strand is bare, and a long stretch of sandy beach divide Three Cliffs from Great Tor. This tower-like landmark is the best known of the Gower tors. It also supplies the most traditional route on the peninsula: the East Ridge. The rock tower itself gives steep and strenuous climbing, while the huge creviced pedestal on which it stands – called Great Flake Wall, and the cliffs immediately above the sands and flanking it on either side, provide a galaxy of routes in every grade. The front wall of the upper tower has yielded unsatisfactory and loose climbs. Its right edge is the East Ridge (240 ft.) which starts from a ledge just above the sea and gives four pleasant pitches of Grade III taking the most indirect line, and Grade V when the walls are taken direct. The left or South edge gives a fine, exposed climb at Grade IV, while round the corner the narrow South facet is V. By starting from the beach on Great Flake Wall it is always possible to make climbs of 200 ft. to the summit of the Tor.

Another carpet of white sand towards Oxwich Bay leads to Little Tor. This beautifully clean piece of rock jumps straight out of the flat beach to a modest maximum height of 80 ft. or so. Only the first 40 ft. is steep and sustained. The centrepiece of Central Flake (IV+/V) is obvious; so is the darkly-stained Scout Crack in the sub-wall to the right. Beyond Little Tor the huge curve of Oxwich Bay sweeps round to Oxwich Point. After passing Port-eynon and its point we happen upon more gems of Gower climbing. The Port-eynon to Thurba Head section of the coast is

35. (left) Eryl Pardoe making light work of the Central Flake on Little Tor, the delightful rockface at the edge of Oxwich Bay sands. Great Tor in the background.

36. (right) Yellow Wall, probably the most classic artificial route in Gower. It bulges continuously for 120 ft., has an unsatisfactory finish, and retreat if late presents problems with the tide and escaping from the small cove in which the cliff is situated at Mewslade.

the most complicated on the peninsula. The good crags tend to be isolated from one another, and situated at different levels on steep ground cut by grassy cwms above the sea. At sea-level the few worthwhile climbs are difficult to locate, and at low water the beach is much broken by large rocks and limestone pavé for four miles. Boiler Slab, near the Port-eynon end, is still the only frequented cliff in this section. There are several excellent routes from Grade III to V+ on splendid rock, including Classic, the first of Alan Osborn's climbs in 1949. White Pillar is the next outstanding piece of rock; the West Kante (100 ft., IV+) is a good example of Talbot's eye for a route on a compact face, leaving little else for followers to discover. After a series of contorted buttresses and ridges, and having passed Paviland Cave, the sentinel-like piles of the Sisters – three in number – are reached along the lower cliff path. The South Wall (120 ft., VI) of the Second Sister by Pardoe and Talbot in 1969 is rated as one of the best climbs on this part of the coast.

The next great headland is Thurba, supported by smooth limestone walls from which the sea never recedes. Routes are now appearing on the sea face and Talbot has climbed the great chimney-zawn in the Mewslade flank. In Gower the near-equivalent of a Cornish zawn is a *slade*. On the far side of Thurba Head lies Mewslade, a small bay under the headland, narrowing towards the tower-like tor of Lewes Castle. Here again is a perfect beach of golden sand. From it rises the most continuous collection of cliffs in Gower, where the highest standards of climbing have been achieved. Only at low tide springs is the beach in its narrowest parts fully revealed. At normal times care is needed not to be cut off. Whereas there are many fairly easy scrambles and climbs to exit from the beach, to be caught by the tide on either side at certain points could prove distinctly awkward. The cliffs are deeply gashed by a maze of chimneys and gullies, while several massive tor-like promontories jut forward into the sands. Among these the White Edge is most imposing; rising to the clifftop path the horizontal summit ridge is narrow enough to daunt tourists from wandering along it for a giddy view of the beach. Similar knife-edge crests adorn the top of Jacky's Tor and Devil's Wall (The Razor).

The climbs at Mewslade range through all grades of difficulty, but everything is steep. Vertical or overhanging cracks and walls like Prima and Kalk on Cathedral Wall are possible at Grade IV+ because of superb holds and rough rock. All over the rocks at Mewslade the limestone has been honed into painfully sharp edges and these can prove most useful in the hands of skilful climbers. Rockfaces are also peppered with shallow holes, like Gruyère cheese, with razor sharp edges. The trinity of routes on the upended coffin of Block Buttress (Cima, Kaiser, Power Trap – all about 120 ft.) epitomise the best climbing at Mewslade up to Grade VI.

On the outside edge of Block Buttress the trade route is South Pillar Rib (140 ft., IV).

Lewes Castle stands at the far end of Mewslade beach. The seaward face rises from a large sloping fault called Great Terrace. Below this is the fine King Wall, falling straight into the sea at high water. Normally at low tide there is just two hours to move along the sand at the base of the wall – though traverses on to the face can be made from the descent route in its centre, called Great Cleft. Practically every route (and there are many) is worth doing. The name of Talbot's original King Route (III) – a nice piece of face climbing – was inspired by his visits to the Swiss Engelhörner, where the Kingspitz is a sought-after summit. The main wall of Lewes Castle is divided by a steep grass recess and a gully. Left of this is the loose South-West Pillar, right of it the longer and celebrated South-East Pillar (120 ft., V). This is also loose but climbed quite often. The two best routes are near the gully; Gethsemane (III); and further right the magnificent South-West Dièdre (110 ft., V+), which for quality is greatly underrated in the present guidebook. Round the corner from King Wall the sheltered beach of Fall Bay is a favourite gathering point for climbers. The temptation here is to sunbathe and swim during the long hot Gower summer. The walk from Rhossili carpark is fifteen minutes.

Off the farthest point of Rhossili lies the much admired but rarely visited Worms Head – a tidal island connected to the mainland by a limestone causeway which can be crossed at normal low water. As it is a good hilly mile to the far end you have to be quick in returning or be marooned for six hours.

A tip for the adventurous newcomer to Gower. Visit Tor Gro on the North side of the peninsula, which rises pristine-like from the vast salt marsh of Landimor. The rock is excellent and clean, with climbs of 150 ft., but take a machete to progress along the foot of the cliff.

8   Pembrokeshire

Access: For Lydstep area: By railway to Tenby, then by bus to Lydstep in 5 miles. For St David's Head: By train to Haverfordwest then by bus in 20 miles to St David's village. No bus service from village along 2 miles of approach roads to Whitesand Bay; taxis.
Accommodation: In Lydstep-Tenby area, ample bed-and-breakfast establishments (list from Publicity Officer, Tenby Council Offices). St David's has similar accommodation in village and more limited facilities at Whitesand Bay.
Camping: Private campsites in vicinity of Lydstep; pitching tents on open clifftops is not permitted (National Trust Land). Private and popular campsite and caravan park open to all at Whitesand Bay for St David's – owner in row of houses opposite.
Facilities: Small and sufficient shops and cafés in Lydstep and St David's. Buffet, public toilets and carpark at roadhead in Whitesand Bay.
Earliest recorded climbs: Tenby Peninsula: 1954. St David's: 1966 (unrecorded climbs before this date).
Maps: O.S. One Inch, Sheets 138, 151. O.S. $2\frac{1}{2}$ Inch, Sheets SM 62, SM 72 (St David's). Sheets SR 89/99, SS 09/19 (Tenby Peninsula).
Guidebook: None. Provisional work in preparation during 1972. Various routes, especially at St David's, recorded in magazines and in *New Climbs* annual during second half of the 1960s.

This county forms the extreme South-West of Wales. The coastline, facing South, West and North across the Bristol Channel, Atlantic, and St George's Channel, is deeply indented by bays and river estuaries. The entire seaboard was designated a National Park zone in 1952 but there is little evidence that the ground is so preserved either in controlled amenities or marking of features of general interest. Geologically it is one of the most interesting coastlines in Britain, with many miles of fine cliff exposure. The rock beds strike more or less West-East with beautiful symmetry in three main groups. Along the South coast between Tenby and Linney Head the prominent sea cliff material is Carboniferous Limestone, though it alternates with Old Red Sandstone. The limestone is simply an extension across Carmarthen Bay of the Gower Peninsula exposures. Inland the North side of this coastal region is bounded also by water, in the long estuary of Milford Haven. There results geographically

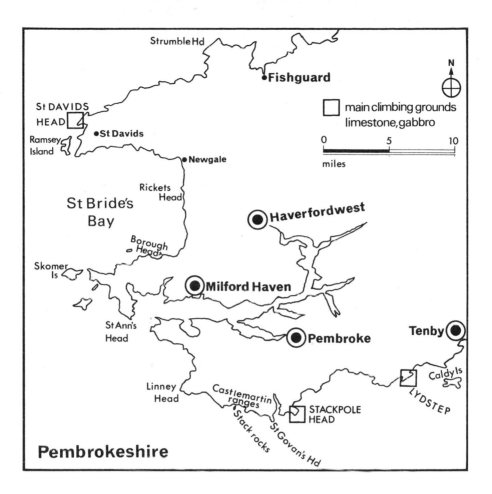

Pembrokeshire

a land mass called the Tenby Peninsula, orientated identically with Gower, almost in the same latitude 35 miles apart and displaying several similar features. North of the Tenby mass is found a central zone of predominantly Old Red Sandstone. This rock occurs frequently on the western seaboard above Milford Haven; the coast winds in and out erratically round the ragged finger-like headlands of St Ann's and Wooltack Point, with large islands out to sea, before resuming a more regular northerly direction along the back of St Bride's Bay. The sandstones give out near Newgale at the North end of this bay, and make way for volcanic rocks filling the projection of St David's. The gabbro sea cliffs of St David's Head and the adjoining Ramsey Island are unique in South Wales and in England and Wales as a whole.

The splendid coastal scenery of Pembrokeshire was little known to the public at large until after World War Two. St David's, as the most

westerly tip of Wales, was always regarded as "remote", and this observation was still being made in the 1950s. In climbing, this headland is generally assumed to have been "re-discovered" in the 1960s, though this can be shown to be merely an event of publication. John Cleare had scrambled there several years previously. Similar claims for the Tenby limestone have been made, but in 1954 schoolboys were active here too, classifying routes and giving names to climbs and coastal features that do not coincide with published nomenclature of later arrivals. A similar situation had arisen in the Chair Ladder area of Cornwall before the War (which was not unravelled until 1951), and Jeremy Talbot can relate parallel experiences in Gower over a shorter period of time.

The sandstone in Pembrokeshire has so far not provided much serious climbing. John Cleare has covered most of it in foreshore traverses of the coasteering style, climbing various isolated cliffs of up to 100 ft. and a few stacks on the way. The major effort has been concentrated at St David's and in the Tenby Peninsula. Both of these areas are now crowded with routes, but with plenty of scope for extending exploration to associated cliffs which for one reason or another have hardly been touched at present. Paradoxically the unsatisfactory historical record of climbing in Pembrokeshire is due to the small number of individuals involved with the early exploration. None of them had cognizance of another working in the area, and significantly the wildest claims are from those most latterly on the scene. This fragmented approach was, and still is, due to the great distance of Pembrokeshire from centres of population – bearing in mind that it has not achieved the category and status say of equally distant Cornwall. Some distances to St David's, for instance, are: Cardiff, 110 miles. Bristol, 150 miles. Birmingham, 230 miles. London, 290 miles. Climbing interest in the coastline emerged incidentally and accidentally, and even today the pace-making and repetitive visits are confined to a handful of enthusiasts.

In dealing with the Tenby Peninsula comparisons with Gower are inevitable. We know both areas quite well and feel confident about our impressions and the predictions that can be made. Firstly the limestone cliffs of Tenby are more serious in several respects. There are generally no beaches below the best cliffs, such as those at Lydstep and Manorbier. They drop straight into the sea, and at low water a blank rockface still remains. Climbing descents can be unpleasant; abseiling to the foot of such cliffs, say to a ledge identified near the waterline, is normal practice. This

37.   The Pembrokes limestone sea cliffs called Mother Carey's Kitchen on Lydstep Point in the Tenby Peninsula.

applies to at least half of the developed coastline, whereas in Gower such tactics are virtually unknown except when parties go in to climb at high water. Putting aside general problems of access, more particular rock features courted by climbers tend to have their own descent routes in Tenby. Lateral movement at sea-level to reach another set of routes may involve a difficult sea traverse. On the highly developed headland of Lydstep this situation governs climbing activity round the central mass of Mother Carey's Kitchen. Further West three or four independent rock masses can be reached from a common descent beside Slab Buttress (originally called White Buttress), where the routes, as might be expected, are less serious, but the well known eastern-end routes on White Tower, with its impressive South wall facing seawards (called Tombstone Buttress originally), and Pinnacle Buttress, become disconnected again by sea-filled chasms.

Then the rock at Tenby is decidedly looser. Some of this must be due to the lack of traffic sustained by the cliffs to date. Gower climbs have been done many hundreds and thousands of times, and besides have benefited from the work of a master-gardener over a period close to 15 years. If sea-washed rock is the guide to soundness, then waves and spray must rise higher along the Gower coast than in Tenby. There is a good 20 ft. difference on average between deterioration levels in the two areas (70 ft. versus 50 ft. in Tenby). Both coasts are savaged by Atlantic gales but it appears that more momentum is gained by waves sweeping over the sloping beaches under cliffs in Gower. The profuse barnacle growth on Gower rock, which provides the only hold at the bottom of some of the smoothest tidal faces, and which takes several hammer blows to remove even the smallest shells, is mainly absent at Tenby. The shifting level of sand against Gower rockfaces could explain this.

Finally the wrinkled surface texture of Gower limestone, like elephant skin, and often pock-marked and pitted with small holes as if the rock had been subjected to gunnery practice, is much less pronounced in Tenby. At Lydstep the "big" climbs are on smoother, looser rock almost immediately above the sea. In Gower you would expect to encounter these characteristics only on the upper series of cliffs. There is no comparable upper series in Tenby. A further point concerning scenic features are the fine caves, natural arches and tunnel systems to be seen along the Tenby coast up to Linney Head. In Gower the famous caves occupied by early man are found in the upper cliffs and denudation of the limestone at sea-level is possibly less marked.

John Cleare and Reece-Jones made the first notable climbs on Lydstep Point in 1962. The period coincides with the first "foreign" invasion of Gower. In the same year they girdled St Catherine's Island off the harbour point at Tenby, and looked at the slanting limestone slabs on Proud Giltar, running East towards Giltar Point. All these give climbs of up to 140 ft., and have been developed more recently by Jim Perrin.

Some distance must now be covered to the West before reaching Stackpole Head where the limestone cliffs again provide a large number of routes. The main headland, and the most southerly point of the Tenby Peninsula, is St Govan's (sometimes Gowan's), which is part of the huge Castlemartin tank and gunnery ranges ruled over by the Army. Hereabouts all the clifftops are flat grassy plateaus standing some 150 ft. above the sea. The ground is littered with blown-up tanks, broken targets, bunkers and the debris of warfare. Access and therefore climbing is forbidden except on certain Sundays during the annual holiday at the range in August. Then two or three lanes are opened to the public, leading to the clifftops. A growing number of climbs are being done all along the coast from St Govan's towards Linney Head, but after the half-way point at the Stack Rocks the coast seems to be permanently closed. This is certainly the longest continuous stretch of limestone cliff in South Wales, with immense potential that may take many years to realise due to the military presence. The absolute debarment of the public from part of it will undoubtedly become a political issue in the fight to assert the rights of way on the Pembrokeshire Coastal Path which is a continuous clifftop ribbon round the county coastline. As in the one round the Cornish coastline it is designated a National Park.

Ten years ago the Germans started coming to the Castlemartin area under NATO arrangements, and since then some 40,000 of them have trained on this range of 6,000 acres. The hostility, which was expressed more by English visitors than the local people, has long since gone. Village shops and stalls are full of goods described in English and German, souvenirs for the soldiers, and reminders of home. However the climbing is entirely unofficial. Anyone caught roping down the cliffs or coming up them with a rope is liable to be marched off to the guardhouse as a suspected spy landed from a submarine. On St Govan's Head there is an area of almost horizontal slabs below the clifftop, similar to Dancing Ledges at Swanage, various pinnacled rocks at sea-level and narrow rocky inlets, such as Huntsman's Leap, which would give excellent climbs. During an unauthorised exploratory tour, Cleare found the way up in a chimney between a pinnacle and the main cliff blocked with old rusty anti-tank shells.

Jim Perrin, Pat Littlejohn and others have done routes at Bullslaughter Bay, about half-way along the seaward edge of the tank ranges. Near the Stack Rocks there is a huge hole about 100 yards across in the flat plateau, a short distance inland from the sea. Its base is connected by a series of

massive caves to the sea. Inside at the bottom is found a subterranean "sea", rough with waves, and cliffs of more than 100 ft. drop straight into it. A number of hard routes have been put up here.

The only well publicised climbing adventure in the Castlemartin area was the duly sanctioned and successful attempt on the Stack Rocks near Bullslaughter Bay in 1970. More correctly called the Elugug Stacks, these are probably the most impressive "sea mountains" outside Scotland. The Elugug Tower is the higher of the two, a massive chunk of rock some 150 ft. high with overhanging walls and a grassy crown of sea cabbage. By contrast the Elugug Spire is needle-sharp and about 130 ft. high. From the cliff edge a 150 ft. abseil from a concrete post down steep walls and over overhangs of tottering shale leads into the dark well of a tiny cove. The two stacks rise beyond the usually heavy surf.

In October a strong team of sea cliff specialists, including Peter Biven, Frank Cannings, Jim Perrin, Martin Hogge, Ian Howell and John Cleare, acted on permission received and went down into the cove. A force eight was blowing on-shore. As it was spring tides they discovered it was possible to cross to the Tower at exact low water fairly safely. A tyrolean was rigged to facilitate eventual escape and Biven and Perrin managed to complete the first steep pitch, about Grade V, before it became imperative to retreat. The cove was a swirl of angry white water and the party beat a damp and hasty escape by climbing up the abseil ropes on jumars. The next day was 1st November. The gale had subsided and the party arrived well before low water. A rope was taken out to the platform from which the Spire rises. Just before low tide Cannings and Howell started work on the formidable West wall. Meanwhile Martin Hogge was trying to recover what remained of the ropes and other gear that had been abandoned in the surf the previous evening. At the top of the fixed ropes Biven led the final pitch to the summit of the Tower, which was not difficult but awkward over poised loose blocks and on to the blowing cabbage field that is the top. The rest of the party had time to join him on the Tower and build a large cairn before Howell and Cannings completed their excellent and remarkably solid climb on the Spire. The Tower route had been pretty obvious but everyone had wondered how the Spire would eventually go – if it would. It turned out to be a master-piece of unlikely route-finding, very airy but well supplied with excellent holds where they were most needed.

Both teams had difficulty fixing abseils to leave their respective stacks.

38.   Elugug Stacks, offshore from the Castlemartin NATO ranges; the Tower (right), the Spire (left) seen during the original exploration in 1970.

The Tower party roped down eventually from a wooden wedge, for cabbage roots are not like those of the mountain ash, and both parties made it safely back to land, if a trifle wet. Off-duty soldiers of a Panzer battalion watching from the clifftop had been impressed.

Beyond Linney Head and the Castlemartin area the great waterway of Milford Haven divides the Tenby Peninsula from the so far least known part of the Pembrokeshire coastline, extending out to Wooltack Point and Skomer Island but generally working North up St Bride's Bay to the large peninsula of St David's. Old Red Sandstone is now the prominent rock, occasionally disturbed by the remnants of limestone. Before the entrance to the Haven large cliffs appear South of Angle village, and on the other side similar exposures lie South of Marloes village. In the area of the neck and narrow strip of ground projecting towards Skomer Island there are impressive but loose cliffs at Deer Park. On the island itself, closely guarded by the Nature Conservancy, limestone cliffs of 200 ft. rise out of the sea. Jeremy Talbot looked at these some years ago, photographed them, and reported that the movement of all visitors is watched hawk-like by wardens. On the southern edge of St Bride's Bay igneous rocks appear on the coast, and a coasteering type of traverse has been made from Goultrap Road round Borough Head to near Mill Haven. The Stack Rocks off this part of the coast have been climbed by Mortlock and Perrin. Along here too the Coastal Path right of way was bulldozed near the cliff edge but is now mostly overgrown. Half-way up St Bride's Bay, Rickets Head has been explored and a mysterious cairn was discovered at the top of the most obvious route line.

Nearly all the southern side of the great St David's peninsula is composed of igneous rocks. There are at least two cliff zones worthy of considerable attention, without access problems or special hazards, which should become popular in the future. These are at the headlands of Dinas Fach and Dinas Fawr, just East of the harbour inlet of Solva village.

Dinas Fach is a small peninsula composed of fine-looking Chamonix-type pinnacles, affording sea-level traverses, good traverses over their grassy tops, and very steep routes on the flanks and on the retaining cliff wall either side of the headland. Reaching many of the climbs depends on the state of the tide and parties should work to the correct time in relation to this, or be prepared to swim or use a rubber dinghy – valuable anyway and easily carried down to a superb little beach. The number of parties who have been here to climb, and who have not so far committed their routes to paper, is such that when Robin Collomb surveyed the area in detail during 1970 he found no less than 17 cairns in a variety of places, marking the start or finish of routes.

Dinas Fawr is a wider, less imposing headland. There is plenty of scrambling or steep rock difficult of access, and not much between the two extremes. Horizontal movements of any distance are complicated by deep zawns.

The outstanding expedition on this versant of the St David's peninsula is the Eldorado Traverse, extending from Newgale Sands to the cove of Porth Mynawyd, a little East of Dinas Fach, and covering a map distance of $1\frac{1}{2}$ miles. It was accomplished after several "serious" incidents by a large party led by Biven and Cleare in 1970. No less than six tyroleans had to be made, two pendules and several zawn-swims. The cliffs are made of various igneous rocks, some good, some bad, but consistently steep and forbidding. Escape routes up or down looked impossible to the party. The clifftop provides no abseil points; you are confronted with a slope of bluebells getting steeper and steeper, merging into vertical or over-hanging rock, in some places nearly 300 ft. above the sea. During the course of the traverse the party crossed round into one zawn, full of deep shadow and smooth blank walls; then with a clatter a flock of white rock-doves flew out of a cave at the back and spiralled up into a shaft of sunlight penetrating deep into the zawn. In May the party suffered from exposure. Constantly taking to the sea, sometimes unintentionally, the cold water was an unpleasant discomfort throughout the traverse. The best time for an attempt would be late August or early September.

The climbing style afforded by St David's Head could not be more different to the southern Pembrokeshire coast. This headland has the over-stretched honour of being the remotest important climbing ground on igneous rock south of Scotland. Climbing possibilities on the headland and on Ramsey Island were noted as long ago as 1900 by A. W. Andrews, O. K. Williamson and others. Writing in the Climbers' Club Journal of 1950, Andrews admitted that during the intervening fifty years he and N. E. Odell "planned a visit and perhaps a guide to the cliffs but circum-stances prevented". It would appear that Andrews never set foot on the faces. The cliffs were undoubtedly missed by other visitors who went on to the actual tip of the headland and found good scrambling. They are effectively screened from most points along the top of the headland by a roof of gorse, and crown the end of a series of short spurs running seawards. C. J. Mortlock, who developed the cliffs after 1966, did so following a paddle up the coast by canoe, which revealed the potential. The rock is gabbro, a coarse-grained granite in bright grey and russet brown. It is not as rough as the famous rock of the Black Cuillin in Skye but the frictional properties are better than the worn crags of Snowdonia and the Lake District. Plenty of natural belays occur though peg stances are taken on some of the harder routes.

St David's, nominally a city by possession of a cathedral, but in fact no more than a small village, is situated about three miles from the Head. Before the Middle Ages the centre was called Menevia. The famous cathedral church in its present form dates from 1180, and has been restored several times since; prior to this there were three earlier edifices and the original dates back to the earliest Christian times. In the Middle Ages the cathedral with the shrine of its founder, St David, patron saint of Wales, attracted many pilgrims, including kings and queens. On the opposite bank of the now sluggish Alun river are the remains of Bishop Gower's palace (1342). The promontory itself is rich in archaeological remains. Evidence of early occupation by man is seen in numerous stone monuments (menhirs, dolmens and circles). An "Arthur's Stone" is situated at the head of the zawn forming Craig Coetan. In the sunken valley immediately inland from the line of cliffs is an example of ancient field enclosures, quite extensive, while the fine lookout peak of Carnllidi above them, now spoiled by World War Two military emplacements, has burial chambers. There is good scrambling on this summit, including a ridge of 300 ft. with Grade II pitches at the start.

The normal approach to the cliffs starts from the roadhead at Whitesand Bay – a large beach at low water, under the South side of the headland, and much frequented by water-skiers. About half a mile outside St David's along the Fishguard A487 road, a fork is taken left on B4583. This leads in 1½ miles to a large carpark behind the beach. A stile on the North side of the carpark marks the coastal path working along clifftops to a small moor on the West side of Carnllidi. A descent follows to stepping stones at the seaward end of the sunken valley, close to a sandy inlet. A track rising across the slope of the headland to the West ends at the tip of St David's. This is taken until the track levels off, then you leave it and walk a short distance North through gorse to the first cliff view. Below lies a rocky inlet and its right-hand wall is Craig Coetan, the first of the four main sea cliffs. The furthest is 1,100 yards away along this North-West side of the headland. Wide scoops of steep grass and rock, ending in zawns, separate these cliff sections, which stand forward into the sea on large buttresses. Intermediate zones of coastal cliff are fairly continuous, of lower height and awkward to reach. A small, partly overgrown path follows the rough gable behind the projecting cliffs, past the coastguard lookout on point 249 ft., but

39. Eryl Pardoe making an entry into the imposing corner of Goneril on the Black Cliff at St David's Head, one of the boldest leads in South Wales.

it is easily lost. The official coastal path follows the sunken valley further inland but this too is hardly visible in places. Working up the coast the four main cliffs are: Craig Coetan (Red Cliff), Mur Cenhinen (Black Cliff), Craig Carn Porth-Llong (Coastguard Cliff), Trwyn Llwyd (Grey Nose Cliff). The local name "Porth" is the direct equivalent of "zawn" as in Cornwall, and the word adopted in climbing vernacular to describe a deep cleft in a sea cliff.

As there are no beaches at St David's, in the terminology of the coastline these are offshore cliffs. Sea-level traverses have been made during exploration but they are of more value as approach or escape routes and are not generally practised for themselves. Granitic rock beside the sea is normally slippery. It attracts seaweed and green slime because it does not have the self-erasing properties of limestone. This is a disconcerting aspect for the newcomer to St David's. Consequently the majority of routes start from ledges and natural traverse lines above the rock affected by the tidal range. One of the delightful aspects of this gabbro climbing is that routes of quality are well represented in all grades. The easy climbs on Craig Coetan are particularly suitable for novices.

Craig Coetan is the only cliff that can be seen and studied from the moor on top of the headland. However the best view is obtained by descending into its flanking zawn, down steep grass, rubble and then on to a spine of perfect gabbro jutting into the sea. Nearly all the climbs start from a slanting rake well above the sea. The lower wall can be partly traversed by another narrower rake. Below this the rockface drops directly into the sea. Most of the climbs are in Grades II and III; the best is perhaps Zigzag (210 ft.). Better still are the harder routes called Central (200 ft., IV+) and Silmaril (200 ft., V). The rake can be followed round the seaward corner of the cliff on to a belt of slabs which descends as a gangway along the base of the formidable West flank of Mur Cenhinen. At low water this traverse can be continued round a slippery rib (III) on to the sea washed ledges under the central black wall and eastern flank of the cliff. This makes one of the most interesting excursions at St David's, for the Black Cliff is the scene of the steepest and hardest routes in the area. The normal descent to the

40.   (left) A typical situation on the fine slabby Red Cliff at St David's, which consists of rough rock covered with pleasant routes on nice holds.

41.   (overleaf) Martin Hogge leading Barad on the gabbro cliffs of St David's Head. This picture looks equally right when turned into a vertical position (incorrect).

eastern part of the cliff is down the opening between the cliff and the Coastguard buttress. After scrambling down broken ribs, a smooth crescent-shaped glacis bends below the East wall and slides into the sea. The rock is often greasy and great care is needed to avoid spinning into the water. In the centre of the cliff, above the end of the glacis, rises a characteristic "Cenotaph Corner", climbed and named Goneril (150 ft., VI/VI+) by Martin Boysen and A. Williams in 1968. This route and another called Barad on the Trwyn Llwyd cliffs are the two great classic lines of the area. Both the eastern and western wings have yielded routes of high quality, mainly inspired by Boysen and Estcourt, giving up to 200 ft. of climbing at Grade VI or harder. Morfran (190 ft., VI) by Mortlock and Webb is classic.

The Coastguard Cliff looks the least attractive of the four main cliffs. It covers the largest area horizontally, and the problem is to find starts low enough to make the best use of the seaward-facing rock. About ten climbs have been worked out. The fourth and final climbing zone is the most complicated: Trwyn Llwyd. It lies below and between twin promontories with ridges running down to the sea, some distance beyond the Coastguard Cliff. The ridges (Grade I or so, and nice while they last) are used to reach several climbs, while in between two or three unpleasant chimneys have to be taken with an abseil descent to reach the centrally located routes. A zawn with steep walls divides the cliff complex, and various projections forming smaller zawns, clefts and caves are exposed or partly submerged along the cliff foot, according to the tidal condition. In the northern section a fine rock ledge high above the sea gives access from the descent ridge to a number of popular climbs. (This descent has actually become polished, though it must have been used by fishermen before climbers.) The best known is Barad (320 ft., VI), pioneered by Barry Webb and C. Baker as early as 1966 and then prosaically entitled Charlie's Darling. The wall of the central zawn flanking the Barad buttress has yielded routes of comparable difficulty and interest. The central and southern climbs are shorter, in grooves and chimneys.

Further up the coast gabbro cliffs occasionally appear in sandy bays. At least two of these have been extensively developed, with routes up to 80 ft., on predominantly slabby rock.

The longest and least known climbs at St David's lie on secluded Ramsey Island, a bird sanctuary about 3 miles across the water South-West of Whitesand Bay, but only half this distance from the hamlet of St Justinian, across Ramsey Sound. A motor launch makes the crossing in summer with day trippers. Special permission is needed to climb or stay on the island, and no climbing is allowed until the end of the nesting season, in early August. As it took Colin Mortlock, the first explorer, eighteen months to obtain his original permission in 1967, and because subsequent parties have been few in number, intending visitors should apply well in advance to the Tourist Office in St David's. The office in turn makes representations to the owners, the Royal Society for the Protection of Birds. There are two sets of cliffs on the West side of the island, Alt Felin Fawr and Carn Llundain, giving routes on gabbro up to 400 ft. long. Some of these have been described by Mortlock as comparing favourably with the better routes in Snowdonia at the level of Grade V, on mainly excellent rock. Details of some of the climbs were published in the old series of *New Climbs* during the late 1960s.

42. (overleaf) Rusty Baillie on a practice roof climb on slate cliffs at Tonfanau near Towyn in Merioneth (not detailed in text).

9 Anglesey and North Wales

Access: For the Anglesey Gogarth and South Stack cliffs, by rail to Holyhead. Walking from the town centre takes over an hour. Unreliable bus service in summer months to vicinity of South Stack café. Most visitors come by car across the Menai straits from Caernarvon or Bangor. The Lleyn Peninsula sea cliffs and those at Little Orme are likely to be visited only in day trips at present by car from main centres in Snowdonia.
Accommodation: None in Gogarth Bay area, but possible by arrangement at South Stack café.
Camping: Sites near South Stack café. Water and meals available.
Earliest recorded climbs: On main Anglesey sea cliffs: 1964. On Lleyn Peninsula and Little Orme, at later dates.
Maps: Gogarth – O.S. One Inch, Sheet 106. O.S. $2\frac{1}{2}$ Inch, Sheet SH 28/38.
    Lleyn Peninsula – O.S. One Inch, Sheet 115.
    Little Orme – O.S. One Inch, Sheet 107.
Guidebook: Crew, P., *Anglesey-Gogarth Climbers' Guide*, West Col Productions, 1969. Guides are projected for other sea cliff areas.

Anglesey is the largest island of England and Wales and is mainly flatter than all the other coastal areas described in this book. It is therefore all the more remarkable that this island in name has attained a unique reputation in British climbing over a period so short as seemingly to make ludicrous the decades of development sustained both in other coastal and inland regions. So much has been written about the emergence of the Anglesey sea cliffs near Holyhead that in this chapter we shall refrain from giving readers a conducted tour of the area and concentrate on putting it into perspective in the context of modern coastal climbing, and will also examine its contribution to and position in British mountaineering.

In our view the national position can be summarised as a prolonged phenomenon. Anglesey stands for the most successful example in Britain of transferring the highest standards of technical achievement on the customary sound rock of mountains, in this case Snowdonia, to a zone of cliffs where the rock is poor or bad, and persevering with the aim to make scores of routes. In the end the psychological barriers posed by loose rock are broken down. Anglesey demonstrates that all the necessary

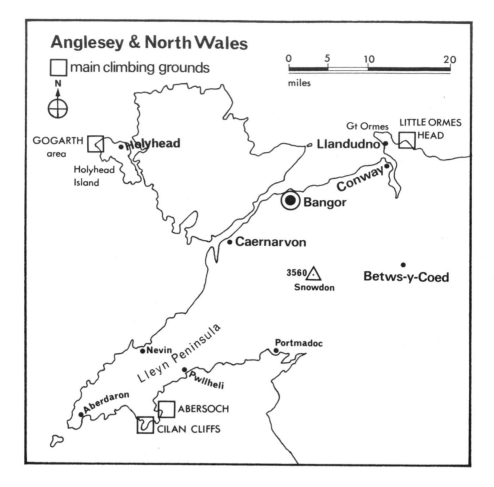

Anglesey & North Wales

☐ main climbing grounds

N

0   5   10   20
miles

GOGARTH area   ☐ Holyhead

Holyhead Island

Gt Ormes   LITTLE ORMES HEAD ☐

Llandudno

Conway

Bangor

Caernarvon

3560 △ Snowdon

Betws-y-Coed

Lleyn Peninsula

Nevin

Portmadoc

Pwllheli

Aberdaron

ABERSOCH ☐

☐ CILAN CLIFFS

confidences have been won. Poor rock becomes good rock by the standards established for the cliffs, and bad rock becomes bearable with extra care.

As we shall conclude, the position in sea cliff climbing is much less definite. Climbing on Anglesey has been largely motivated by the desire to extend the scope of Snowdonia mountaineering. The cliffs have the length and steepness of the most serious crags in the central mountain area. Fairly reliable weather encourages all-year-round climbing. Until quite recently the incentive of finding a good new route was a bonus that could be counted on. That Anglesey climbing is done on *sea* cliffs – and offshore ones at that, with no beaches, was a situation to be borne bravely and not shunned. Despite the maritime surroundings the record clearly shows that exploration took place in the landcliff idiom. It reveals completely an extension of attitudes and practices adopted on mountain crags.

43.   *The Rivals from Nevin beach on the North side of Lleyn Peninsula. The nearer sea cliff is of limestone, while the outline of the main volcanic cliffs on the mountain, situated above the sea, appears behind.*

On this subject Biven has written: "The development of Gogarth illustrates the basic difference between the southern sea cliff climber and the northern crag climber. The Anglesey cliffs were developed by crag climbers who were looking for the vertical way up. Even now the sea level traverses are not complete, because the sea was seen as a threatening and alien environment. Swimming to a route was rare, abseiling the norm; accident victims were hauled up the cliff and not taken off by boat; benighted climbers, of considerable repute, were prepared to sit it out rather than take to the water which is common practice in the South."

The matutinal spirit of conventional rock climbing, occasioned by a walk of an hour or two, sometimes more, to a high North-facing crag, vanished with the advent of Anglesey. Visitors get there at midday or early afternoon, when the sun is highest and the sea breezes are voluptuous. They merely have to stroll across grass bands for a few minutes to the cliff tops. However in the heroic days (only five years ago!) the stroll was replaced by a scramble to beat other parties in the "rat race" to collect new climbs. Open competition flourished between climbers on these cliffs. Subterfuge in passing on information, laying false trails, inventing non-existent routes on horrible pieces of rock were common ploys pressed into service by rival parties. One contestant held a pack at bay by clinging to the first pitch of a potential new route for three hours, moving slowly up and down 30 ft. of rock, unable to get higher, until an overdue companion arrived to take up the lead. A performance reminiscent of Brown on Resolution (no, not the Llanberis one) deserves to be reported in a better set of circumstances. Though pundits in the Welsh school, championed in the publicity field by Ken Wilson who had focused attention on Anglesey in a blaze of photographic light, denounced such behaviour, it was accountable in most cases to and symptomatic of the dissipation ruling among an amorphous group of climbers living in the Llanberis district, or attributable to other climbers deeply influenced by association with the Llanberis movement. The extremes of conduct witnessed on these cliffs have no parallel in British climbing history. This disaffected group of people formed for the first time in a mountain area a commune of a type not unfamiliar nowadays in large cities with overcrowding and work problems, and young people rebelling against social order and the establishment. In their fundamental

44. Joe Brown (leading) and Peter Crew on Rat Race, Gogarth Main Cliff — so named because several parties and numerous climbers were in the running before the first complete ascent was made.

desire to escape from the claustrophobic cities, from nine-to-five jobs and attendant responsibilities, and live in the mountains, they became in time estranged by a veneer of poverty and aimless purpose in life from the surroundings they admired and wished to preserve.

Anglesey happened notably because the potential for big routes was drying up on Clogwyn du'r Arddu. This most famous of all post-war British climbing grounds had dominated ambitions of greater and lesser climbers for a long time. Technical achievements on the steep blank walls of Cloggy progressively reached new heights through the fifties and sixties, spurred on by the masterful performances of Joe Brown. Finally Cloggy became the only cliff in the country to have an entire book published about it. Some time before this event a lassitude in purpose had descended over elements in the Llanberis "movement". Climbers were heard complaining openly of boredom. They preferred the hard and insecure living of keeping up with competitors in some new trend or development with general recognition. Approval in this sense could be an example set by one climber. Following a fashion, sheep-like, and keeping in step with rapid changes as in pop music, are afflictions in modern mountaineering caused by closer alignment with normal society. In the mountains it is increasingly difficult to escape the subtle pressures that publicity and advertising exercise on attitudes and actions. In the psychiatrist's paradise of Llanberis and Deiniolen, development had become patchy, the consumption of beer rose in bars now commandeered and degraded by unruly climbers, and energies were expended in various unsavoury directions commonly pointing to a catch-phrase of the age; the permissive society. Previously, and on a much smaller scale, misfits in mountaineering had generally acted with stylish discretion but the scene now was thoroughly squalid. Drugs were circulating and the police were making inquiries about a multitude of misdemeanours and attempting to catch the culprits.

Against this disquieting background the sea cliffs of Anglesey entered the public domain with a loud fanfare of trumpets in 1966–67. These are quartzite cliffs, very uneven in texture and quality even for that rock. The pre-Cambrian series of Gogarth Bay is older than the volcanic rock of Snowdonia. Quartzite is a metamorphosed sandstone, the grains having been welded together under great pressure. The rock is not so good as the better known series dominating the Twelve Pins in Connemara, where

45.   Spider's Web, a climb in the Wen Slab area of Craig Gogarth. Joe Brown is seen leading to the outer lip of the cave arch forming this sensational route.

it is also smoother and scarcely fissured. But Anglesey after all is a sea cliff and is more exposed to constant frontal denudation. It was the friable rock and bottoming in water, and not the situation, which is fine, that kept away all but a few enthusiasts until 1966. But then the vanguard also had a penchant for secrecy which was fairly well preserved so far as where there were climbs to be found for a further twelve months.

The B.B.C. staged a television show at Easter, 1966, using a particularly loose piece of rock called Red Wall on the South Stack cliffs for climber-actors to demonstrate their powers and skill. Most climbers were still apprehensive or cynical about the permanent value of the climbs now being put up, and Joe Brown could be numbered among them. But when Brown turned his attention to the cliffs with customary determination a few weeks later the road to a glory hole of new routes of a high standard and quality became clear by the end of the year. It need hardly be said that where others failed Brown succeeded. At the age of nearly forty he repeated the run-away performances he had given on the mainland during his twenties.

Sea cliff climbers – dare we say of the true breed – like Biven, Cannings, Littlejohn and a host of others do not hold Anglesey in high esteem. Possibly they resent the reasons why the cliffs have become so popular. Or as one put it: "Anglesey is no place for a sea cliff." There is little scope for any except the most proficient climber. But Biven has admitted that events on Anglesey, including the less palatable ones, have served to accelerate the popularity of sea cliff climbing. The cliffs were fine while the rush to make first ascents was taking place. They became a national talking point. They re-confirmed that developments in North Wales could still lead progress on a national front. The coastal location was played down, the benevolent weather and masses of vertical rock on which to grip yourself were extolled. A prime feature of the cliffs was the sea, and climbers went there despite it and not because of it. It can be argued that there is no need to annexe sea cliffs to a northern play-ground. While there is always plenty of rock for the majority frequenting mountains, the avant-garde movement in the pastime today is constantly having to cast its nets in all directions as the last pieces of virgin rock are married off to persistent suitors. Except in quarries and in ground producing a lot of outcrops, cliffs of the necessary size, solidity and steep-ness can only be found along our shores. In this scheme there is an eternity

46. Laurie Holliwell leading Tyrannosaurus Rex, a fairly new and exceptionally fierce route in the Wen Zawn on Craig Gogarth.

of distance in the outlook between the northern crag climber and southern coastal climber. To be the latter, and do it well, you must be an incurable romantic. According to Biven "the most seductive quality of sea cliffs is the extension of childhood seaside activity – hunting in rock pools, beachcombing among the Squeezy bottles, and half expecting to find, in the dank recesses of the zawns, the bloated bodies of drowned sailors".

Some doubts have been expressed for several years as to whether the main climbing grounds of Craig Gogarth and the South Stack Cliffs on Anglesey would survive the test of time. Some said they would soon be forgotten; they were surely freaks which temporarily attracted the wilder instincts of the vanguard. Peter Crew, who wrote the guidebook, hinted as much for the future. The cautious forecasting for Anglesey has proved unnecessary. Publicity given to the southern sea cliffs, and the growing number of expeditions to stacks and greater headlands in the North of Scotland have carried Anglesey on a tide of rising interest and entertainment. It was awarded a second television programme by the B.B.C., though only when some of the local Welsh "stars" turned their thumbs down after reconnoitring Torbay as an alternative. It may seem after all that if parties in North Wales are prevented from climbing on Cloggy by bad weather they will go to Anglesey.

The great concave main cliff of Craig Gogarth is just about the only face on Anglesey that can be reached down to sea-level by a scramble. You can also work along the foot of it at low water for more than half the horizontal distance without meeting difficulties. It is also possible to enter Mousetrap Zawn without rope tactics, but everywhere else entails abseiling, often tricky, as in Easter Island Gully, the Wen Slab Area, and on the Red Wall, Castel Helen and Yellow Wall sections of the South Stack Cliffs.

Sea cliff climbers are now travelling all over the country to visit or explore new coastal areas, in the same way that mountain areas near or far are attractive. But Anglesey remains an extension of Snowdonia, unlike any other sea cliff zone, and climbers normally go there because it is part of Snowdonia, with its strong and lively mountaineering activities. Even so the surroundings of Gogarth Bay are too austere and the climbing too serious to impart to the cragsman more than technical satisfaction. The modes of entertainment and communion with the sea – suggested in the Introduction to this book as qualities the sea cliff climber looks for and feels – cannot be conjured up on Anglesey.

The word used against southern cliffs is that they are "fun" climbs. The fun is supposed to be that you can frighten yourself on short hard climbs in safety, and at worst only fall into the sea. The gulf in understanding is thus wide.

The rest of North Wales as the rock climber regards it consists of the Lleyn Peninsula. In the search for new crags a flurry of activity commenced inland in 1966, and this quickly led to exploration of the coastline. On the North coast the twin summits of Yr Eifl (The Rivals), which have large faces standing above the sea, but which are not strictly sea-washed cliffs, yielded long climbs as far back as 1953. One of these early routes is undeniably classic: Avernus (800 ft., IV+). But it was the South coast that produced a crop of climbing grounds, though none of them appear to have been treated in the sea cliff idiom. They were looked upon as rockfaces on which new routes could be put up to compensate for the deficiencies of Snowdonia. An assortment of steep faces are strung along the coast between Aberdaron in the West and Pwllheli in the East. Except on quarried faces, such as those at Tyn Towyn near Llanbedrog, the rock tends to be poor. The Cilan Cliffs at Abersoch, about 250 ft. high, are the most extensive group, and development is in an advanced stage. To date all of these cliffs have eluded

47.   The limestone cliffs on Little Ormes, seen from Great Ormes across the bay in front of Llandudno.

favour. They are of course more distant from the central areas of Snowdonia than other places a climber retires to in bad weather, such as Tremadoc; or Anglesey for that matter. The Lleyn Peninsula sea cliffs seem unlikely to achieve recognition either as good sea cliffs or worthwhile options when the mountains are out of condition. By contrast the new mainland climbing in the Lleyn, especially on the Rivals and further down the coast at Nefyn (Nevin), in a semi-mountainous setting, and with the sea only as a backcloth, is gaining in popularity.

The first truly characteristic sea cliff to emerge in North Wales mountaineering is the Little Orme (correctly Little Ormes Head), the lesser in stature of the twin limestone headlands between which the resort of Llandudno shelters. The eastern promenade curves towards the cliffs. So far as can be ascertained Joe Brown and Peter Crew made the first attempt to reach the cliffs. They were repulsed and returned with the story that "they were crap". Subsequent exploration unfortunately does not give the impression that this view was reached too hastily.

A huge nose forms the tip of the headland, and promised a spectacular climb; getting to it was the problem. After the end of the promenade the cliffs dropped into deep water for most of the way along to the distant nose. In March 1968 Frank Cannings and a companion found a grass band fault leading on to the cliff about 100 ft. above the sea. This was traversed until they had to rope down into a small cove with a back beach. A line of prominent chimneys offered a way out to a band of compact cuboidal limestone, getting steeper higher up and leading to bad grass 450 ft. above the sea. The party attempted this route but was stopped by a ferocious looking colony of cormorants. This drove them to use an exit from the cove which has become known as the Easy Way Up, or Off. It gave 200 ft. of climbing mostly on grass and terrible rock pitched at 85°, up to a terrace christened the Seagulls' Fish and Chip Shop, covered with guano remains and old bones. The party continued upward for two more pitches, with peg and free climbing, taking a grass overhang and with holds frequently restricted to the roots of a rare wild cabbage. Finally, from an area of steep grass, the team was obliged to escape by making a tension traverse to safety from an anchor secured to one of the cabbages.

Later it was discovered that sea birds nesting on these cliffs present a serious hazard to climbers. Moreover, the Nature Conservancy, having been advised that climbers were romping about on the cliffs, lodged a protest with the local authority for the breach of privacy being caused by the intruders. The matter does not seem to have been resolved.

When news of the first exploit reached Peter Biven, he and Mark Springett demonstrated the speediest method of reaching the little cove by swimming out to it. Meanwhile Cannings was again trampling across the cliff to the same spot. Both parties made new routes, to the right of the Easy Way Up, which joined higher up on the face. These lines took clean steep rock near an overhanging black wall and were called Thorfin Scull Splitter (Biven) and Rhiwledyn (Cannings). The latter is the local name for the cliffs, corresponding with "Gogarth" on the Anglesey cliffs.

Attempts were now made to reach the elusive nose from the far (East) side of the headland. Within a few days of each other two parties managed to make a sea-level traverse of considerable interest for 400 yards and only of Grade III towards the nose. Both were stopped at the edge of a small bay guarded above by a smooth concave cliff of 200 ft., on the East side of the nose. Cannings found a way up the side of this barrier and crossed the top of it to set foot on the nose. It was altogether disappointing, having one of its flanks composed of steep insecure grass. The tantalising profile seen from a distance was merely picturesque, and the hopes of explorers pursued for some months had proved false. The other party (R. J. Isherwood and K. J. Wilson) escaped upwards from the traverse in a very loose gully. This was such an appalling climb that neither of them returned to the cliff.

A situation now arose where all the main contenders retreated from the scene, except Roland Edwards. With considerable determination and ingenuity, plenty of risks and by all accounts coming within an ace of breaking his neck, he proceeded to make a series of artificial lines up the concave cliff using almost entirely pegs and bolts, sometimes with a companion but often working on his own. The approach technique was entirely by roping down from above, and leaving fixed ropes in position to assist an escape if the event arose. He has also worked on other parts of the cliff. The abundant loose rock and steep rotten grass on the upper tiers, the unpleasantly delicate or rope-down descent approaches, coupled with official opposition to climbing, combine to dim the future for the Little Orme. In any case a small boat seems to be the best method for making a landing on the cliffs.

10   Northern England

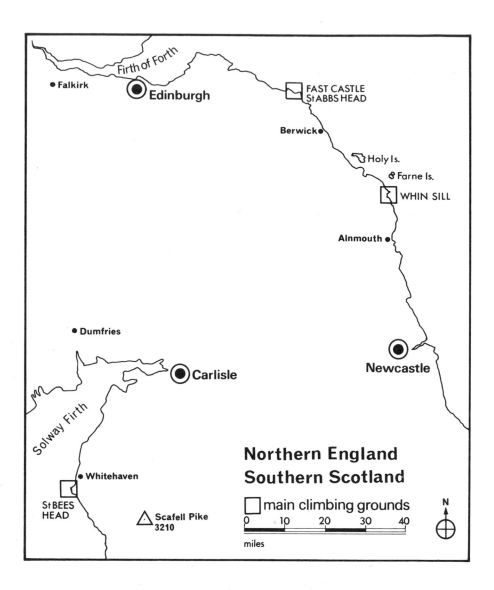

Northern England
Southern Scotland

main climbing grounds

0   10   20   30   40

miles

N

Firth of Forth

Falkirk

Edinburgh

FAST CASTLE
St ABBS HEAD

Berwick

Holy Is.

Farne Is.

WHIN SILL

Alnmouth

Dumfries

Carlisle

Newcastle

Solway Firth

Whitehaven

St BEES
HEAD

Scafell Pike
3210

West Cumberland is one of those doubtful industrial zones, not large enough to make the headlines in times of economic depression, and not so small as to escape the notice of conservationists. The real industry is varied but well contained. The atomic energy works at Seascale – some distance South of the Workington-Whitehaven complex – has come in for more criticism. This coastal zone divides the Lake District from the sea. As such it has never been visited by many climbers. The mountain valleys opening on to the plain, West and North-West, are still the least frequented in the Lakes area. Indigenous climbers in West Cumberland, always few in number, invariably travelled eastwards to their climbing grounds. There are stories of a few characters pottering about on the coast. As far back as 1894 Haskett Smith relates of St Bees: "Several accidents have occurred on the cliffs here. They are of sandstone, and incline to be rotten. The height is only about 250 ft. The Rev. James Jackson (the self-styled 'Patriarch of the Pillarites') lived at Sandwith close by, and was fond of climbing about on these cliffs."

By 1967 publicity given to sea cliff climbing in the South was having a marked effect on the psychology of looking for new cliffs all over the country. In this year the first climbs were recorded on St Bees Head, by local people and later by a few visitors who may have been slightly disappointed.

The headland lies a couple of miles beyond the outskirts of Whitehaven. The North Head, below the lighthouse, is easily accessible. About $1\frac{1}{2}$ miles away the South Head is closer to St Bees itself – a small town. Between the two the coast is nicked by the small haven of Fleswick Bay, of southerly exposure and a sun-trap. Coming out of Whitehaven you have the interesting juxtaposition of driving up a steep hill through the Marschon Chemical Works then twisting down a quiet lane and through a farm to the lighthouse poised on the edge of all things, looking across to Snaefell and the Isle of Man rising distantly from the sea. Some steps cut in the cliff below the lighthouse lead down to the sea. At the cliff bottom there is no sight or sound of the industrial city. Bits of jetsam washed ashore and fishing boats passing up the coast are the only reminders of the commercial world.

The cliffs are of very steep New Red Sandstone and the rock is intrinsically sound. They could be described as a "Super Harrisons" – being about five times as high as London's famous sandstone outcrop, and nearly three miles long. The cliff wall, vertical or overhanging, with huge roofs and bold towers, resembles one side of some great canyon in America. At low water it is possible to scramble along the boulders and slabby rock at the bottom all the way to St Bees. The first 1,000 yards are completely tidal and the usual precautions must be observed to avoid being marooned on the cliff. After Fleswick Bay and the Three Castles section the cliffs towards South Head appear to be less interesting, though we understand that routes of over 300 ft. have been made here.

48.   (below) Profile of the Old Red Sandstone cliffs at St Bees Head.

49.   (right) The first pitch of the route called Jimarten on St Bees Head.

The average is about 200 ft. Although the cliffs are impressive the whole place is lacking something in character – that is in the sea cliff idiom. Horizontally bedded sandstone is fairly monotonous to look at. The experienced sea cliff climber will miss the more broken coasts of Cornwall and Gower, and the gleaming white and yellows of the limestone areas. The rock itself also communicates an austere feeling, alternately soft and hard as the feet pivot on friction holds and the body wriggles strenuously in jamming up holdless cracks.

It soon becomes apparent that easy routes are hard to find on these cliffs. Most of the natural lines climbed to date, and these are nearly all cracks, look deceptively easy, but none has been graded below V—. Jimarten, the route photographed for this book, was pronounced Grade III on inspection from the bottom. When the party finished it they were in a somewhat ruffled condition and had a great deal more respect for these gigantic Harrisons' problems with gritstone overtones. A number of large horizontal breaks across the rockface assist in the completion of some routes. More *demi-tours* have been done at St Bees than on any other sea cliff we know because the top layers of sandstone could not be climbed, and the absence of traverse ledges left or right prevented parties from finding exit prospects on another part of the face. At present routes are concentrated in the first cliff section of 250 yards between the lighthouse steps and a tower gap called Lawson's Leap, and on the buttresses called Three Castles some way south of Fleswick Bay. More climbs are being put up on other parts of the cliffs, but even now only a small proportion of their full extent has been touched.

A pamphlet guidebook is available locally; eventually it is planned to include St Bees Head in one of the Lake District guidebooks for climbers.

Across thirty-five miles of the Irish Sea from St Bees lies the Isle of Man. Its central mountain mass of Snaefell is noted for the Manx slates series. A fair amount of sea cliff exploration has taken place sporadically over the years. This can be pin-pointed in the southern part of the island, mainly in the South-western extremity round Spanish Head and on the Calf of Man, an islet detached from the main island. Slate cliffs of 200 ft., rent by chasm and fissures, lie just South of Cregneish. On the Calf of Man are probably the finest sea cliffs in the Isle of Man. Access is difficult because of a strictly kept bird sanctuary. Several impressive sea stacks adorn the area, which is uniformly traversed by igneous dykes. Further east, in the Castletown area, a zone of Carboniferous Limestone has basaltic intrusions which enliven the coastal scenery. Climbing on

50. The second pitch of Jimarten.

the Isle of Man was documented up to 1960 in a small booklet which is no longer available. So far as we are aware no details of modern sea cliff climbing have been published.

In the first chapter on the Chalk of Southern England it was noted that apart from the picturesque bird-infested cliffs of Flamborough Head the East coast of England is poorly favoured with cliff scenery. In the North-East, in County Durham and Northumberland, several interesting coastal features appear. Most of these have been explored by climbers but nothing worthy of detailed description has been found. At Marsden, a few miles outside South Shields, there is a striking beach stack, called The Rock, consisting of well-bedded magnesium limestone. It resembles the most imposing of the needle-stacks in sandstone in the North of Scotland. This rock and the cliffs to its rear, about 100 ft. high, now give several hard climbs. Further South and close to Hartlepool are Blackhall Rocks. On the beach is another stack, rather dumpy, of dolomite rock standing on a brecciated reef. This has almost certainly been climbed.

Moving North across the Tyne estuary into Northumberland we enter the Great Whin Sill country. The whin is an intrusive igneous rock, a quartz dolerite or basalt, dark in colour and exceedingly tough. It makes excellent roadstones and outcrops at points along the coast from north of Alnmouth to Bamburgh. The Farne Islands off Bamburgh have great cliffs of the whin. The whole group belongs to the National Trust and is preserved as a bird sanctuary. Visitors are normally banned.

The Whin Sill coastal cliffs were first developed by Peter Biven during his national service in Northumberland in the early 1950s. The main outcrops form promontories, as at Cullernose Point and Castle Point (Embleton). There is also a worthwhile band of cliffs between these two points. The columnar structure of the whin, up to 80 ft. high, provides a host of vertical faults in cracks and chimneys. At Castle Point the whin rests on horizontally bedded sandstone, giving one style of climbing at the bottom and another quite different in the middle and top. Dunstanburgh Castle stands behind the Point, and this draws attention to several ancient monuments from the Middle Ages that were built upon the whin either on the coast or somewhat inland. Despite a relatively powerful climbing population in the Newcastle and Teesside areas the coast has been largely ignored.

51. The third pitch of Jimarten.

11   Southern Scotland

Over the border at Berwick-on-Tweed the North Sea coast develops into a tract of wild rolling moorland, reaching its apogee in a bulge of two headlands called St Abb's and Fast Castle. Old settlements, hill forts and ruined castles decorate this zone along a hill-crest guarding approaches from the sea, from Telegraph Hill to Oatlee Hill and Bell Hill. The hill-flanks drop directly to the sea and give the highest cliffs in Eastern Scotland, up to 400 ft. of rock in places. The coast is very contorted and of great interest to the geologist. The rock is a kind of dolerite, black, compact and very hard; there are also patches of a grey-white friable shale. The cliffs have been severely folded, resulting in an amazing variety of inlets, caves, clefts, skerries and stacks, and one coastal waterfall. Several small lakes huddle in hollows behind the hill ridge, giving additional isolation to the sea cliffs. The remote atmosphere of the headlands, reached by tiny roads across a commonland which supports a few rough farms, reveals an exciting coastal area of the kind sought after by dedicated sea cliff climbers.

The St Abb's Head area is within easy reach of Edinburgh, and Newcastle climbers have also made their mark in the neighbourhood. The Fast Castle end of the cliffs was the first object to be investigated by climbers, in 1965. Gordon Davison and Jack Binns made a series of routes here which were written up later and distributed as a pamphlet. (This pamphlet, though now much out of date, has been reproduced verbatim in the new Southern Uplands District guide, published in April, 1972). The castle ruins are perched on a narrow crag of black dolerite jutting out to sea. Directly below the ruins is a 200 ft. cliff where the original routes were made. Further South a cliff nearly twice this height has yielded more climbs on vegetated rock. Ledges on the Fast Castle cliff are liberally covered with guano and climbers frequenting the area in the nesting season may experience considerable discomfort in this respect. From the cliffs there are fine views north towards the Bass Rock, the Firth of Forth and Isle of May, and the Fifeshire coast. Access to Fast Castle is by car to Dowlaw Farm. You park below the farm beside a line of old cottages, then take a signposted field path to the castle ruins. James IV, King of Scotland, once said of the owner "only a reech meanie man wood live in a castle as mean as that one". The castle is also feigned to be the Wolf's Crag of Scott's *Bride of Lammermoor*.

A mile East from Fast Castle along the poor and often overgrown

52.   *The ruins of Fast Castle on top of its cliff, looking down the coast to the emerging Souter stack a mile away.*

clifftop path you reach The Souter. This is a dolerite stack of 120 ft., the top of which can be seen over the nearby crags from Fast Castle. It stands in a shallow box-like ravine, enclosed by igneous dykes which are so conspicuous on this lonely coast. An easy scramble down the back of the ravine and boulder hopping in the bed leads to the base. The boulders are uncovered until half-tide. This elegant pinnacle was first climbed by D. Bathgate and R. Campbell in 1967. Their route meandered over the landward and eastern flanks and aid was used. The climb has been done about half a dozen times. In 1971 Cleare and Howell climbed the seaward face by a straightforward and direct route to the top at Grade V. One peg for belaying and another for protection were used. The summit is tiny and a pleasantly free abseil takes one down to the bottom. The cliffs here abound with good scrambles. Round a corner from The Souter and across a cove where a narrow glen with a stream drops into the sea lies The Brander. This is a long dyke, rising up to 40 ft. and jutting into the sea for several hundred feet. A traverse of its ridge gives an excellent scramble over narrow pinnacles, but you have to return the same way. Climbs have been made on its flanks. Further South and East down the coast development is moving apace on the initiative of Edinburgh climbers. St Abb's Head is described as the "best climbing hereabouts". The cliff below the fort on Great Pitts has potential for routes of 500 ft.

There are indications that sea cliff climbing in Southern Scotland, and further North on the Aberdeenshire coast, may become a cult in the Scottish mountaineering movement. Already it serves an immediate purpose as alternative sport when the Highlands are shrouded in mist and rain. Bad conditions in Scotland are so frequent that keen rock climbers living in densely populated areas like Edinburgh can quickly acquire the habit of going to a milder coastal region. This is happening at present at St Abb's Head. At the very least a new dimension is being added to Scottish climbing, which will play a not unimportant role in the Scottish scene of the future.

53. (left) The 1971 route on the seaward face of The Souter, near Fast Castle Head.

54. (over) Roping off the top of The Souter, showing the landward side of the stack where the original route was climbed.

12   Aberdeen Coast

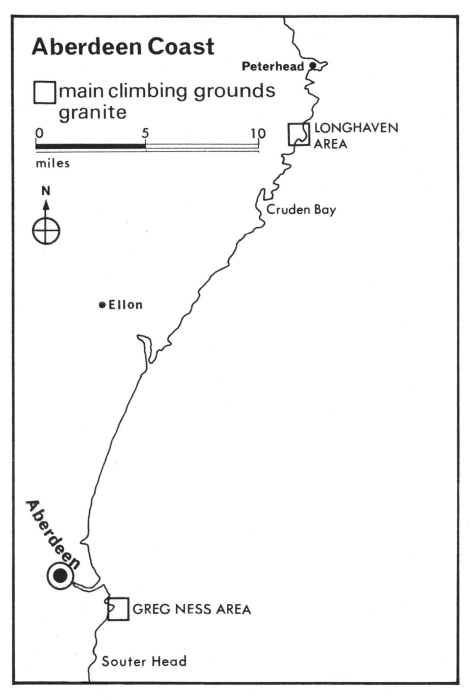

Aberdeen Coast

☐ main climbing grounds granite

0 ─── 5 ─── 10
miles

N

● Peterhead

☐ LONGHAVEN AREA

Cruden Bay

● Ellon

Aberdeen ●

☐ GREG NESS AREA

Souter Head

Aberdeen is a city built in granite. Great quarries where the stone was hewn from the ground can be found among abandoned ruins on the bleak coast of the North Sea. A purely local movement of long-standing among Aberdonian climbers has developed this granite coast extensively. It may surprise some that climbing activity began in the 1930s, totally in isolation and unconnected with similar stirrings in the South. The coast was used as a nursery and practice ground in preparation for the rigours of mountaineering in the Cairngorms and other parts of the Highlands.

The city and surrounding landscape of Aberdeen are unrestful on the eye; there is an emptiness about the scenery, a loneliness and isolation, and sometimes a coarseness which are discouraging to the stranger. We are not aware of more than half a dozen parties from the South who have made a special visit to the Aberdeen coast in the last ten years, and no report of climbing has appeared in a southern journal or magazine. The Aberdeen countryside is not far enough North to excite the spirit of exploration, as in Sutherland or the Islands, and in long journeys to the North it is not only overlooked but its existence is unknown. This region is a populated wilderness, almost treeless, with small farms and stone walls, wind-swept down to the edge of the low coastal plateau.

Above and below the city the coast is formed by a broken complex mass of granite cliffs. The quarrying in these was generally done a few yards inland so that the stone was not taken off by boat. The result is that several prominent inland coves or hollows, water free, have been created, and these as well as the natural cliffs facing the sea are climbed upon. The rock varies a good deal in colour, from red and salmon pink to grey. Most of it is very rough with large coarse crystals. Some of it is in fact gabbro, the roughest of all. The longest stretch of coast of interest to climbers lies immediately South of Peterhead. The main road (A952) comes close to the cliff-edge at the big sea inlet of Longhaven; from here to the next headland, Murdoch Head, are found the best routes along the Aberdeenshire coast. Some of the most popular climbs lie in the Longhaven quarries, parallel to the coast and connected in series by crater-like depressions. The climbs reach a maximum height of 200 ft., as on the Red Wall, and give remarkable exposure on satisfying holds. All the cliffs in this area are broken by dozens of inlets and little zawns

55.   (previous page) Perdonlie inlet on the Aberdeenshire coast.

56.   Two local climbers on Alligator Crawl, the trade route in the Perdonlie sea cliff area just South of Peterhead.

154

with fine buttresses and towers dividing them. The Longhaven quarries are almost immediately followed by another fine series of walls and flying buttresses either side of the Perdonlie inlet. A disconcerting sight in these coves is the rubbish tipped into the back of them. The head of Perdonlie is a dump for old cars trundled over the clifftop by disenchanted owners. The sea-level traverse of the inlet is classic and 400 ft. long (III); it is usual to finish up the Edge (150 ft., III). A continuation line, Zwango, is much harder (V) and opens the way to further traversing possibilities. The Longhaven coastal area ends in the pleasant sweep of the Grey Mare Slabs where all the routes are covered with large rough holds.

On the southern outskirts of Aberdeen coastal climbing runs from Greg Ness to Souter Head and a little further – a section we have not been able to examine for ourselves. The longest climbs do not go up much more than 100 ft. and they were first explored in more recent times.

On the Aberdeen sea cliffs we were reminded of the stories told of what it was like to climb on the Derbyshire gritstone during the 1930s. The economic depression enabled out of work young men to climb all week on the outcrops a few miles outside places like Sheffield and Chesterfield. With this kind of practice they reached in a short time a high technical standard, but only a few of them were fortunate enough to find the means of putting their skills to use in the mountains. At the Perdonlie inlet two young lads came to the cliff-edge and were slightly puzzled as to 'our presence. It was mid-week, they were out of work and had nothing better to do than climb. So what was our excuse. Half a hundredweight of photographic equipment and a generous pile of climbing gear gave the game away. Cleare was recognised when one said, "I know you" – meaning that he must be that southern photographic chap who went around the country taking pictures of climbers who had been persuaded to pose for the camera in distinctly risky situations. They thought it must be a grand life compared with their own restricted activity. However they did not know that Cleare had been telling some of his working companions recently that it was costing him £50 for every picture eventually published in a book or magazine, such is the high percentage of waste in this kind of work. You exposed a couple of dozen rolls of film in one trip of perhaps more than 1,000 miles for the round journey to a secondary climbing location (like the Aberdeen coast!) and might find the publication opportunity to use three prints. He was not doing it to stick photographs in an album, as one postal inquirer presumed; he wanted to visit the

57. Perdonlie Edge, an easy ridge climb used as an exit from the classic sea level traverse of Perdonlie inlet.

offices and browse through the pages for something to stick on his living room wall. The two young lads quickly realised that they could help with our problem, and obliged us by pointing out a vantage point from where we could watch them climb a route called Alligator Crawl – "a tribute to the late Fats Waller, being smooth and in the groove". This was the best climb on the cliffs round the corner from the Perdonlie inlet. The young men got away without us learning their names.

One can see how a coastal area in remote Aberdeenshire has reached such a high state of development without making an impression on southern climbing movements. Communications in mountaineering between Scotland and England have always been bad. At the moment, in the early 1970s, they are as bad as they have ever been. The Scots keep to themselves, probably resent the intrusion of successful "raiding parties" from England who forage in the North and come away with some prize that provokes unmerited publicity, and silently lament the injustice that proper recognition is seldom given to Scottish achievements, both at home and abroad. The rise of competition in mountaineering worries the Scots, as those in England are mainly responsible (there are notable exceptions!). Scottish nationalism in every sense divides ways of thinking between the variegated masses in the South and the parochial, clannish bands across the Border. It can be seen as the familiar situation of a majority invading the self-asserted privacy of a minority. In an age of social and common services being sought for a nation as a whole, in a country described as the United Kingdom, the part of it called Scotland reacts independently on all possible fronts. It is fair to say that militant views held in Scotland are responsible for keeping the two so far apart in mountaineering matters. On the other hand the "popularisation" of certain Scottish areas would spoil the atmosphere of an original and adventurous landscape. Trends in the South are moving towards central organisation in mountaineering on a national scale, to achieve improved services for the individual. In this process we are merging with the European Economic Community and bureaucratic rule, all of which strikes anathema in the hearts of Scottish individualists.

It is refreshing to find a granite littoral so different from the more familiar Cornwall and Lundy. There is more greasy rock at sea-level in Aberdeenshire, but in spite of this traverses have been cultivated as a natural outcome of climbing on sea cliffs. Traverses are possible

58. Diagonal Crack, one of the best routes at Longhaven Quarry, taking an exposed line up the Red Wall section of the cliffs.

because of more continuous rock, natural horizontal lines and an abundance of holds. Technical difficulty is seldom of a high order on the Aberdeenshire coast. Hard routes tend to be made on sea cliffs if mountain crags are a great distance away. This is not the case at Aberdeen; difficult routes tend to be short and vicious and fill in much larger areas of climbable rock at an easier standard which is respected as a none-too-serious practice ground. Many areas are still vegetated and dirty; in the South these would have been gardened and cleaned long ago. In the context of Scottish climbing there is no good reason to rectify this situation.

The pre-war approach to these cliffs was only as of a Londoner's interest in Harrison's Rocks for training, as the nearest rock outcrop to home; in Aberdeenshire the coastal climate helped as well. The outcrop "outlook" is particularly prevalent and the Aberdeen cliffs are not yet loved for themselves as are their Southern counterparts. The current guidebook, issued by the Etchachan Club, includes remarks such as "rope work and belay technique can be learned" . . . "judgement and route finding ability on the part of the leader is called for" . . . "a rope cannot be thrown from the cliff with alacrity" . . . "a little loose rock may crop up here and there, but it will at least teach the climber to test his holds carefully" . . . and so on. Observations like these never appear in descriptions of southern sea cliffs, which are potentially dangerous and unsuitable for training purposes. The southern standard as to what constitutes bad rock would also shock the Aberdonians.

The documentation of climbing on the Aberdeen cliffs has been treated more casually than elsewhere. In the post-war revival Tom Patey was one of the prime movers, and he had begun making routes by 1950. Patey was so different in his approach to mountains and choice of companions from the majority of Scottish climbers that his contribution to sea cliff climbing is examined more fully in the next chapter, where sea stacks predominate and stand like monuments to his name.

13 Sutherland and the North

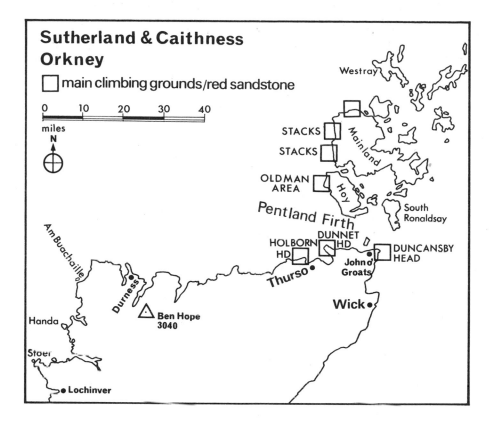

Sutherland & Caithness
Orkney

☐ main climbing grounds/red sandstone

0   10   20   30   40
miles
N

Westray

STACKS
STACKS
OLD MAN AREA

Mainland

Hoy

South Ronaldsay

Pentland Firth

Am Buachaille

Durness

HOLBORN HD
DUNNET HD

DUNCANSBY HEAD

Thurso
John o' Groats

Handa

Ben Hope
3040

Stoer

Wick

Lochinver

Anywhere North of the Great Glen and on the Islands off the West and North coasts of Scotland there are acres – even square miles – of unclimbed rock. In the mainland mountain areas it does not seem likely that many more great crags will be discovered, though some of the Islands may be concealing hidden treasure. Climbing on mainland crags in vogue at present is limited by access over considerable distances, lack of accommodation and fickle weather. Camping in the Northern Highlands can be a serious affair, calling for expedition tactics, and it is not recommended in winter. Many smaller crags may yet be discovered, and the end of this century may still not see an end to them.

If the inland crags are still in a formative stage of development, then the sea cliffs of Scotland's northern seaboards are almost virgin ground. In some complexity the region has the most continuous high sea cliffs in Britain. The predominant rock in the true North and North-East is Old Red Sandstone. This is formed in either thick beds of conglomerate or in thinner layers of flagstone stacked like piles of playing cards. There are untold miles of it, mostly unclimbed and in most places seen only by a few climbers.

Volcanic cliffs make up much of the fine coastal scenery of the inner Western Isles. Even on the Isle of Skye there are sea cliffs on a scale to challenge the famous Black Cuillin ridge and its rockfaces, where the footage of recorded climbing routes is as dense as anywhere in Britain. At Waterstein Head the cliffs are 700 ft. high, unessayed so far, while those at nearby Neist Point have a few routes, including an inshore pinnacle called the Green Lady. Several sea pinnacles off the coast of Skye have attracted parties; the most notable of these are the basaltic McLeod's Maidens, of singular appearance but of no great height (207 ft.). Similar sea cliffs on the neighbouring island of Rum can provide more climbing than its roof of mountains. The late Ian Clough realised the possibilities of Rum and no one seems to have come forward to carry on the work. All the inner islands off the West coast abound in climbing potential. Sporadic exploration has been taking place for some time in parts of Mull, on Islay at Mull of Oa, at Sanna Point on Ardnamurchan, and moving north to the East coast, along the seaboard of Morays, where the sandstone fringes are encountered.

Yet all these widely dispersed explorations are secondary to the potential of Sutherland and Caithness. Of lesser importance to date, the East and North shorelines of Caithness, demarcating two of the county's three boundaries and extending in the shape of a seven for about 100 miles, are almost truncated by continuously splendid Old Red Sandstone cliffs. While the Cretaceous Chalk of Southern England is the most surprising sea cliff builder in Britain, the sandstone is more impressive and extensive. It is the last and oldest of the sedimentary rocks exposed along our shores, and marks the approximate limit to which stratified rock is modified appreciably after it was first laid down. In general the rock is not greatly disturbed and faces the sea with horizontal or but slightly inclined bedding. Frequent jointing at right-angles, in a vertical plane, affords an opportunity for the sea to penetrate the rock

59.   *The originator of stack climbing in the North of Scotland, Tom Patey, seen after climbing Am Buachaille – in the background.*

162

and wear away softer material trapped in the bedding and joints. The outstanding features of all erosion in Old Red Sandstone are the chimney-like sentinels called stacks (stacs), and the eaten-away cavities, recesses, caves, holes, inlets and many other kinds of indentation all generally classified as geos, which correspond to the Cornish zawn.

The East coast of Caithness, up to Duncansby Head by John o' Groats house, has continuous bands of sandstone cliff ranging from 100 to 200 ft. high, interrupted by shorter stretches of the Caithness plateau falling to sea-level and sandy beaches as in Sinclair's Bay. Only at the top of this section has there been much climbing development. The famous Duncansby stacks are supposed to have been ascended by drunken Norwegian sailors, but the accounts of climbers working at the Dounreay Atomic Energy plant are more reliable. This North-East tip of the barren plateau, enclosed by a line drawn between Thurso on the North coast and Wick on the East, is the most thoroughly explored section of Old Red Sandstone. On the northern side the headlands of Dunnet and Holborn, like pincers round Thurso, provide longer cliff climbs and an assortment of stacks – among them the well-known Clett Rock.

The adjoining county of Sutherland, forming the North-West tip of Scotland and tapering to a point at Cape Wrath, brings us into a landscape of ancient and complex geology. The Torridonian Red Sandstone, which is generally rougher and sounder than the Old Red, is the material that concerns us along the coasts. All the cliffs are higher than those of Caithness. The coastline is honeycombed with narrow sea lochs, and the peninsula-like masses between them are filled with mountain ridges. At many points these terminate in precipices and rugged headlands, while beautiful bays alternate between them. Many people consider the coastal and mountain scenery of Sutherland the finest in Britain and we are in accord with this view. Moreover this inspiring scene provides the background for the most interesting developments in sea mountaineering in Britain.

Along the wild stretch of northern coast between Thurso and Tongue, the main road passes from Caithness into Sutherland. After the Kyle of Tongue the first great headland of the county is formed at the end of the Ben Hope ridge in the remote shores of Whiten Head; this is severed from the Durness peninsula further West by the Lochs of Eriboll and Hope. There are vast unexplored cliffs on Whiten, involving several miles of walking from the nearest road. In a group of offshore stacks

60.   Tom Patey leading the final pitch on Am Buachaille, with Ian Clough below.

which must be reached by boat stands The Maiden. Here in 1970 Tom Patey fell to his death from a mishap when abseiling after making the first ascent. Patey was the most original explorer and climber on the Scottish scene for twenty years after the Second World War. His record of first ascents in Scotland is unsurpassed, and he has left his mark as far away as Devon and Cornwall. He carried this originality to the Alps and the Himalayas, but always he returned to his home base in Ullapool, where he worked as a general practitioner in medicine, to rove in the lonely tracts of northern Scotland, searching for the new experience in mountaineering adventure. His feats in winter climbing – for he was a brilliant craftsman on snow and ice – must rank as his biggest single contribution to Scottish mountaineering. There are many other facets to his achievements, but the initiation of the sea stack surely comes second. When he started to explore the wild coasts of Sutherland he was drawn at once to the virgin summits of these pinnacles which proliferate in the region. Individual enterprise is a necessary driving force in progressive mountaineering, and Tom Patey showed more individualism than most. His style was also coupled with an ability to mix and harmonise with the extremes of other movements and personalities in mountaineering. None more so than those flourishing South of the Border. His companions were often English and parties frequently travelled several hundred miles to join him in his exploits. The outcome of his cosmopolitan nature is that Tom Patey occupies an ambivalent position in the annals of Scottish mountaineering, which is enjoyed and remembered with more affection in the South than the North.

From Whiten Head on the North coast things begin to happen. In the jaw of the parallel Durness peninsula to the West is a curious outcrop of old Cambrian Limestone. This is split by the Great Cave of Smoo, a pothole draining into caverns leading to the narrow cave inlet. Peg routes have been put up round the mouth of the cave. After Durness there is a ferry across the Kyle to join the tiny moorland road running to Cape Wrath. Huge cliffs fall from the trackless escarpment to boulder-covered shores – at Clo Mhor, 600 ft. high and over 800 ft. in the corner of Cleit Dhubh, the highest mainland cliff in the United Kingdom – all, so far as we are aware, unclimbed at any point. Tom Patey and others have made attempts in the past. The rock is Archaean Gneiss and Torridonian Sandstone in a formidably steep wall. Access is difficult and it is really necessary to take a small boat down the coast to reach the

61. Patey and Clough climbing the Old Man of Stoer on the West Coast of Sutherland.

bottom comfortably. However parties who have got this far have then found themselves in the middle of exploding shells, as the vast cliff frontage is used as a target for gunnery practice by the Royal Navy. This is not a mistake you make twice in sea cliff exploration! Cape Wrath itself is only 370 ft. high and several climbs have been recorded. There is no land between this point and the North Pole.

To the South of Cape Wrath, down the West coast of Sutherland, lies the classical domain of sea stacks where Tom Patey pioneered the way. The hinterland is without roads or tracks and there is no coastal path. In the first mile rise the stacks called the Old Man and Old Woman, though the only climbing done here has been on the coastal cliff itself. After six miles a beach is reached, with sand stretching for two miles, which is acclaimed by those who have been there as one of the finest in Britain and easily the most remote: Sandwood Bay. At the southern edge of the bay Am Buachaille, The Shepherd, stands 220 ft. high and is one of Patey's finest discoveries. Two alloy ladders lashed together, and carried over the hills for four miles, were used to bridge the swirling channel between the rock beach and the platform on which the stack rises. Patey used ladders for approaching several sea stacks because he was not a swimmer. To reach the scene of his next major "conquest" we must visit the famous bird colony of Handa Island, some distance to the South, and off the coast near Scourie. He crossed to the summit of the Great Stack of Handa along a 600 ft. rope fixed from the clifftop on either side of the zawn enclosing the rock, and drawn tight in the middle across the summit. This Tyrolean traverse feat covered a distance of 150 ft. along the rope at a height of 350 ft. above the sea. The summit had already been reached in 1876 by a similar rope manoeuvre in which the first man crossed relying entirely on his own strength, hanging to the rope from hands and crossed feet. In 1969 the stack was climbed for the first time in a conventional manner from the bottom reached by boat by Hamish MacInnes and party.

The Old Man of Stoer, near the Point of Stoer headland above Lochinver, is Patey's best known sea stack. When it was first looked at heads were shaken in grave doubt, and there was the local reputation that it was impossible to climb. On the first ascent in 1966 Patey reached the base with his ladders and the party was completely surprised by the splendid rock and moderate technical difficulties. It is one of the easiest of the major Scottish sea stacks (Grade IV+). The climb has become so popular that parties on rock climbing courses organised by mountain training centres make regular visits.

By focusing attention on the sea stack, Patey not only introduced a new kind of objective to mountaineering in Britain, he revitalised the romantic

168

essence of the pastime which had been going stale for decades. It is true that those who followed in his steps tended to use brutal tactics to achieve their goal; but such techniques that may be considered proper for the ascent of sea stacks need not detract from the special pleasures felt by those drawn to sea cliff climbing. In their nature sea stacks are inclined to pose unusual maritime approach problems and give hard climbing on suspect rock. Because they are different, so the scope of sea cliff climbing is increased, and this becomes the great attraction. Nothing is further removed from conventional mountaineering.

14 Orkney and the Islands

In the Orkney islands the mountainous features of Hoy stand in striking contrast with the rest of the archipelago – consisting of some sixty-eight islands. It is composed of massive sandstone beds, and along its West coast these are exposed in magnificent cliffs which generally exceed in height any on the mainland across the busy sea lane of the Pentland Firth. In the northern section of this coast the Old Man of Hoy (450 ft.) is the tallest sea stack in Britain and consequently the best known by name. However it should not be thought that Hoy alone reserves the chief climbing interest. Five other relatively important stacks have been climbed, and four of these are on the main island, called Mainland or Pomona. Public services to the Orkney islands, and internal communications between them, are quite good. Apart from a long journey (though possible by air) the approach to these stacks is less arduous in terms of expedition planning than many a jaunt conceived in the Northern Highlands.

After a certain amount of preparation on the lower pitches for the final climb, the first ascent of the Old Man of Hoy took place on 18 July, 1966. The party was Tom Patey, R. Baillie and C. J. S. Bonington. The route went more or less up the East face – the landward side – and the climbers gave it an artificial grading of A3. In his researches Patey had uncovered the fact that 300 years ago the Old Man did not exist. It was merely a narrow, gigantic promontory jutting from the straight line of cliffs along the coast. About 150 years ago large portions of this had collapsed in rockfalls, leaving a great arch linking the outer end with the main cliff. Finally, about a century ago the remains of the arch crumbled and left a monolith intact upon the beach. The poor quality of the rock in the first two-thirds of its height on the landward side is attributed to this recent formation. And from this it might be concluded that further modification to its shape could occur before the end of the present century – though it seems that this could now only take the form of a collapse that would remove much of its distinctive character.

62. A party with Joe Brown out in front on the Castle of Yesnaby during the first ascent of this stack on the West coast of Mainland, the principal island of Orkney.

Following the first ascent, Tom Patey was solely responsible for persuading the B.B.C. to film an outside television broadcast of another ascent. This programme was mounted on a grand scale and the whole effort seemed to come from Patey's enthusiasm. Apart from climbing teams that would be featured in action in front of the cameras and drawn from the cream of British rock climbing talent, even technical assistants for the assault, load carriers, called "sherpas", and most of the persons helping but unseen on the television screen were mountaineers of repute. So it was that the most powerful publicity medium known to man brought the news of climbing on Hoy directly into the homes of the public. It is perhaps no accident that very little information had been circulated about the first ascent before the TV programme was put out in 1967.

During the television ascents the movement of climbers on the East face cleared away much of the loose rock and the route is now fairly solid, well protected and graded VI – possibly less. The programme also filmed ascents of the South face and South-East arête – much harder and involving a variety of artificial climbing techniques. Since then the ordinary East face route has been climbed more than a dozen times. One ascent was made by a boy of nine who, with his father, disappeared later in an attempt on the Matterhorn. This incident brought forth a lot of fatuous comment from the press. While the technical difficulties of climbing the Old Man of Hoy are not great, getting down safely by the process of abseiling requires great care in keeping to the proper descent route directions; otherwise you come to the end of the rope either with no landing ledge or dangling in space well away from the rock.

In a sense the exciting climbing on sea stacks in the Orkneys has been spoiled from the start by its mode of introduction to the mountaineering world and public at large. From the outset it fermented a competitive spirit and an attitude of "love them and leave them". One commentator has already spoken of the stacks on Hoy and Mainland as having been raped. Some sense of order, logic and historical balance in the course of exploration of these and all other major sea stacks in Britain will be achieved when John Cleare publishes his guidebook to *British Sea Stacks*.

Two miles North of the Old Man the coastal cliff on Hoy reaches its greatest height at St John's Head, about 1,140 ft. above the sea and just about the biggest in Britain. Tom Patey had picked out a line on it. His idea was to sail down the coast in a rubber dinghy and land on the

63. The Old Man of Hoy from the sandstone cliff behind, showing the infinite number of rock layers in which the cliffs are built.

rocky boulders below the cliff. Unfortunately he did not live to carry out the plan. Meanwhile another contender for this big wall, E. Ward Drummond, succeeded in roping down the cliff in a series of hair-raising episodes before reaching the bottom, and spent the next five days climbing up again – to the delight of readers of the *Sunday Telegraph*. This was Ward Drummond's second route on the cliff. Though undoubtedly a magnificent and courageous exploit, the scaling of St John's Head is reckoned in sea cliff climbing circles as an error of judgement and a gross waste of effort. It seems perfectly possible to traverse the boulder beach towards the cliff. This method of approach coupled with using inflatables to float equipment down the coast would enable an assault party to arrive fresh and set up a base of operations at the foot of the wall. The reporter, Anthony Greenbank, who is an experienced mountaineer, later revealed that he found a scrambling route down the side of St John's Head which would have made his job much easier and far less dangerous.

Several miles of cliff above and below St John's Head and the Old Man, rising as at the Kame of Hoy to 950 ft., but averaging 500–600 ft., are riddled with interesting features and await investigation. All of it is characteristic Old Red Sandstone of the upper series with brittle rock and much debris. New routes will need intensive planning in the matter of equipment and tactics and a lot of care in execution. In time they would become solid and desirable targets for parties visiting the islands.

The West and North coasts of Mainland, immediately north of Hoy, present a similar but lower rugged coastline. Here, in 1967, Joe Brown and others climbed the Castle of Yesnaby, aided by members of the B.B.C. television team from the Hoy saga. During 1970 another party took North Gaulton Castle in hand, using elaborate rope techniques similar to Patey's method for reaching the top of the Great Stack of Handa (see previous chapter). A month later Stack o'Roo yielded to a swimming approach in the best sea cliff tradition. In August 1970 the important stack known as Standard Rock off Costa Head fell to a pair of young men called Roberts (no relation to each other) from Caernarvon. It is worth recording the achievements of their visit to the Orkneys. They first climbed Stackabank on South Ronaldsay, a loose, serious but not very tall stack linked to the mainland at low tide. The following day they crossed this small island to climb the easier Clett of Crura stack. Two days later the party made the second ascent of Stack o'Roo, up in Mainland, "only severe but grotty". Next day it was the turn of the fine

64. Close-up of a climbing position on the Old Man of Hoy, showing the shallow horizontal cracks, sand coated, and brittle rock with rounded edges.

65. (below) Artificial climbing by Dougal Haston on the South-East arête of the Old Man of Hoy. A section where several bolts are used.

66. St Kilda. Tom Patey prospecting on the perfect gabbro cliffs near Dun channel, Hirta.

67.   The 1,100 ft. unclimbed wall of Conachair, dropping in a series of large overhangs from the highest point on St Kilda.

shark-fin shaped stack called Standard Rock, recalled above. Reaching it involved a difficult abseil followed by a swim of nearly seventy-five yards to the pinnacle which was climbed by its landward edge without great difficulty. Two days later the second ascent of North Gaulton Castle was achieved. Finally they marched up to the Old Man of Hoy and dealt with the East face in five hours. An unprecedented tour-de-force!

One other group of islands has interested sea cliff climbers in recent times: St Kilda. The Hebridean complex holds a multitude of possibilities, but to look at these would be tantamount to pure speculation at present. St Kilda is the most isolated island group, lying in the North Atlantic 50 miles beyond the Outer Isles in the approximate latitude of Rockall – the last rock between Britain and America. The Nature Conservancy and the National Trust must be consulted for permission to go there. In the current situation a climbing party (less welcome than ornithologists, for instance) would also require military permission and co-operation. A further deterrent is that you have to cross the worst seas in British coastal waters, which only good sailors might tolerate. The main island, called Hirta, is garrisoned by a detachment of the Royal Artillery, working in communication with the guided weapons range on Benbecula in the Outer Hebrides. There is no harbour and all landings are across an open beach. As some of the lesser islands are proportioned like huge stacks in their own right, to explore the archipelago in detail is dependent upon having at your disposal a seaworthy power boat with a tender. The famous cliff of Conachair on Hirta was reconnoitred for climbing possibilities by a strong party including Tom Patey and Joe Brown in 1970. The intention was to stay three days. Because of the weather and mountainous seas they were marooned and a boat was unable to take them off for nearly three weeks.

Conachair is one of the highest sea cliffs in Britain, approaching 1,200 ft. The rock was believed to be gabbro; that is to say, the party had been hopeful of finding a route line constructed of solid material. It turned out to be various gneisses and basalts, being igneous rocks inclined to looseness. The gabbro is confined to much lower and broken crags nearby; it also crops up in other islands in the group in better quantities.

The 1970 exploration party examined the cliff and concluded that a massive effort in artificial climbing would be needed to scale it. The logistics of the approach and progress up the face were terribly intricate. At one point the cliff was overhanging 300 ft. above deep water and huge caves. Another section revealed 500 ft. of steep slabs that might be holdless. Endless bolting was forecast. The slabs ran up to a line of roofs

cut by evidently loose, overhanging grooves and chimneys exiting to the clifftop. "Aye, well it's a gripping place", was Joe Brown's off-hand summing up.

When the islands were inhabited long ago there was something of a tradition in climbing on St Kilda. The sea cliffs were scaled by the crofter population to gather sea-fowl and their eggs. This food was a staple part of their diet. Manhood initiation rites consisted of making specific climbs in different parts of the archipelago, often in bare feet and with a crude hemp rope. Patey established that some of these men climbed on filthy rock with no protection at a standard of difficulty at least equal to our Grade IV. There have been quite recent ascents on the outlying island rocks of Bororay, Stac Lee (544 ft.) and Stac an Armin (627 ft.). While the Old Man of Hoy can be regarded as the highest sea stack in climbers' terminology, the latter two are island stacks and considerably taller. Their cliffs are covered knee-deep in places in stinking guano, and thousands of fulmars and gannets have taken possession. On the rare occasions when it is possible to effect a landing an ascent might be made by the beastly native expedient of beating a trail up the rocks by sweeping with a long stick and slaying the birds where they stand.

68.   (previous page) Rope manoeuvres on the East face of the Old Man of Hoy, with the immense cliff of St John's Head behind – one of the highest rockfaces in Britain, 1100 ft.

69.   Bororay and Stac Lee (left), two of the remote outliers of the St Kilda group. Stac Lee is the second highest sea pinnacle in Britain (544 ft.), after Stac an Armin (627 ft.) also in the St Kilda Group.

Postscript

The development of sea-cliff climbing, as we have seen in the preceding chapters, has been rapid, reaching – as it were – a crescendo in the late sixties, but the symphony is young yet. We make no apology that some of these chapters will be out-of-date by the time they are published. Even while proofs were being read word was trickling through of fresh attempts on our highest mainland sea-cliff, the Clo Mhor, which has repelled repeated attempts by climbers of the calibre of Tom Patey and Paul Nunn. We do not yet know the outcome, but we can be sure that if it is not climbed today it will be climbed tomorrow.

Especially out-of-date will be the chapter covering the north coasts of Devon and Cornwall. These last twelve months (writing in July 1972) has seen this long and wild shore yielding up many secrets to the unheralded exploration of a few silent south-western experts. A new concept of what constitutes bad rock has enabled young Pat Littlejohn to power his way up incredible new lines, often of very unusual character, on such high and forbidding cliffs as Tintagel Head, Pentire Point, Lower Sharpnose and Blackchurch. And on occasion the rock has been surprisingly sound! Littlejohn, his name hardly known in more main-stream circles, must now rank among the top ten rock-climbers in Britain today.

Worth watching too is his companion on many of these climbs, fellow Devonian Keith Darbyshire. Belonging to the first real sea-cliff generation Keith has never climbed north of the Thames – let alone in Wales! He romped up the North Face of Les Droites in a very fast time last year, his first Alpine season. So sea-cliffs too can breed real mountaineers, and surely many more sea-cliff men will by-pass Snowdon en-route for the Himalayas. The wheel has turned full circle since the old pioneers practised for the big mountains on the chalk séracs of Beachy Head, but for many climbers, captivated by the edge of the ocean, sea-cliffs will always be an end in themselves.

Index